Andrew

STEEL T

STEEL TOWN CATS

by

CELIA LUCAS

Illustrated by

Susan Cutting

TABB HOUSE

First published 1987
Tabb House, 11 Church Street, Padstow, Cornwall

Printed by A. Wheaton & Company Limited, Exeter
Typeset by Quintrell & Company Limited, Wadebridge

For Christian, Ruttisaing, Laura,
Sally, Sam, Jack, and Alexander

CHAPTER ONE

WHEN the steel works closed people were not the only ones to suffer. Hundreds and thousands of worker cats, who had who had laboured for years to keep the great factories and founderies free of mice and rats, were made redundant.

This is the story of one cat, Madoc the Magnificent, who refused to accept dismissal with his fur lying down. He was determined the lives of these innocent and industrious animals would not be ruined and he made it his task to find a way out.

It was a cold February day. The wind blew from the north across the wide estuary, whipping up hillocks of grey waves and sending birds, that had come to winter there from even colder places further north, scurrying for their nests.

The same wind, unbroken as yet by the high mountains of the interior, sent sharp darts of cold piercing through the thick winter coats of the 215 cats that were assembled for a mass meeting in the factory yard.

"Friends and fellow mousers, ratters of renown!"

The voice of the enormous black cat with the snow-white waistcoat, white nose, and long, curling white whiskers rang out in resonant miaows across the yard. It was the voice of Madoc the Magnificent, mouser supreme.

"I have bad news for you. The blow has fallen. Our works are to close."

A hiss of shock ran through the group. They'd heard rumours, of course, that something like this might happen but somehow they always thought, in the end, the great steel plant that employed so many people as well as cats would be saved.

"But what are we to do? Where are we to go?" cried a tabby mother of six kittens.

"Can't they transfer us to some other plant? We'd work just

as hard so long as we got our daily rations," said Rufus the Ratcatcher, who was dark ginger with a single splodge of white on his nose. And a low growl of assent greeted his words.

"No, Rufus, I'm afraid not," said Madoc. "All over the country works are closing and we won't be the only redundant animals by a long tail, isn't that so, Patchwork?" Madoc turned to his second in command, an animal with a coat of so many colours that when he lay down he looked more like a rug than a cat.

"Yes, grrr," answered Patchwork. "Our works here in North Wales is only one of many to go. There'll be thousands, possibly millions, of cats out of work, all wanting jobs."

"Couldn't we go into domestic service?" Snowy Tom raised a paw. He was a portly animal, fond of the good things of life, and he had always fancied himself sitting snugly at a family hearth, lapping up bowls of cream and polishing off the Sunday joint. Unfortunately he was also rather smelly and his once snow-white coat was a dingy shade of grey. But he dreamed of comfort and luxury and being waited on by doting humans. "It would seem the ideal solution to me," he said, licking his lips at the thought. "Domestic service, a useful and a happy life."

"No, Tom, be realistic," said Madoc. "We're half wild. However nice the idea seems, you know in your heart we'd never be able to live in people's homes. We're not pets, we're workers. It's bred in us and no amount of wishful thinking will change that."

"I'm housetrained," said Katie Cat, who, like Madoc, was black and white but a lot slenderer. She also had two white paws whereas Madoc's were all black. "I was a domestic cat once, you remember, until my family went away and I got lost and joined you. I'm sure I could get used to it again."

"Yes, Katie, I think *you* could if we could find you a home, and kittens, of course, could be trained at an early age into domesticity, but that's not the solution for the majority of us."

"We could organise ourselves into teams of mousers and go round the country offering our services," said Esmeralda, a grey with emerald eyes who was known as the Efficient. She was never happier than when she was organising other animals but sometimes her keenness was greater than her efficiency.

"If we were people we'd get redundancy money and social security," grumbled Geraint the Growler. "The State would look after us. But all cats can rely on is a few charitable handouts. It's not fair."

"Neither is life," Madoc rebuked him sternly. "It's no good moaning about what we don't get. Let's put our best paws forward and do something. Now, here's what I suggest."

The cats were all attention, ears pricked forward, whiskers erect.

"We get up a petition," Madoc continued, "and we march with it to Downing Street, in London, to see the Prime Minister. We've proved what good mousers we are and there must be hundreds of places where our services are needed. Who'll follow me? Who'll come to London?"

"We will, we will," roared the cats in unanimous growl. "Forward the Purrs!"

"Right, *iawn*," said Madoc, who, living in North Wales, was, of course, bilingual. "We march. *Rydyn ni'n ymdeithio!*"

Then, because he was a poetic cat who had won the bardic crown at an Eisteddfod – which, in case you didn't know, is a Welsh festival of music, poetry and song – he broke into verse:

"Fellow mousers, ratters of renown,
Don't take this with your fur lying down!"

And the cats, led by Patchwork and Rufus, responded in miaows and growls:

"Fellow mousers, ratters of renown,
No, we *won't* take this with our fur lying down."

"Three purrs for Madoc the Magnificent, mouser supreme," cried Patchwork. "Miaow, miaow . . ."

"Purr," the cats responded.

"Miaow, miaow . . ."

"Purr."

"Miaow, miaow . . ."

"Purr."

CHAPTER TWO

THE next few weeks saw the cats busy with arrangements. Patchwork dispatched underdogs – who, as you may know, are mongrels who carry messages for cats – to tell groups of mousers all over the country of their plan and invite them to join the march.

"We'll all meet on Primrose Hill which is just a few miles north of Westminster," Madoc told his followers. "Then we'll march from there to Downing Street in one great body of moving fur and swaying whiskers. How many do you reckon we'll be, Patchwork?"

"At least 5,000," said Patchwork. "Cats are coming from Scotland, from South Wales, from Tyneside, Yorkshire, Cumbria and the Midlands. And they've all agreed to pawmark our petition."

"*Gwaith da*, good work! *Ardderchog*, excellent!" said Madoc. "Now, how about our marching song?"

Carlo the Caterwauler, a slim black cat with long, sensitive whiskers, stepped forward.

"I've composed something, Madoc. Would you like to hear my choir of caterwaulers sing it?"

"Yes, Carlo," said Madoc. "*Diolch yn fawr*. Thank you. Go ahead."

Carlo waved a white paw – it was the only white on his otherwise coal-black coat – and twelve young caterwaulers stepped forward. You could tell they were nervous from the way they all turned round to give their fur a quick lick.

"Right, lads," said Carlo, holding his white right paw aloft like a conductor's baton. "One, two, three . . ."

And to the tune of 'Men of Harlech', the caterwaulers burst into song.

"Steel Town Cats we'll fight like tigers,
Sabre-toothed and claws well sharpened,
Spit and scratch and snarl and bite
And we shall win the day!

For we are the mousers,
Mousers bold are we,
Stretch your paws, extend your claws,
And raise your hackles high!

We shall show them we mean business,
They will ask, whatever is this?
March with us, oh brave young purrcats
And we shall win the day!

Steel Town Cats we'll fight like tigers,
Sabre-toothed and claws well sharpened,
Spit and scratch and snarl and bite
And we shall win the day!"

"Very good, Carlo, *da iawn*," said Madoc when the cats had finished. "That's got just the right spirit and it's an excellent marching song. Now go and teach it to the others. I want them word-purrfect by tomorrow."

"Right," said Carlo. "*Dim problem*. No problem." And motioning his choir to follow, he set off to find his pupils.

"Now, Patchwork," said Madoc, turning to his trusted lieutenant, "I'm going to see our friend Sam. He's been made redundant, too, and I know he'll help us. You remember how he brought us food during the strike a few years ago?"

"Yes, purr I do," replied Patchwork. "We'd have starved to death without him. And what about his greyhound, Miss Kip?"

"Yes, Miss Kip, a splendid hound. What about her?"

"Well," said Patchwork, "she's always been one of our best friends, too. Perhaps she could come with us in case there's anything that needs to be done in a hurry. She is, after all, the Fastest Paw in the West."

"Good idea, *synia' da*," agreed Madoc. "I'm sure we can persuade Sam. I'll be off there straight away."

CHAPTER THREE

DAWN was breaking in the cold wintry sky as Madoc squeezed himself through the tall gates at the entrance to the works complex and made his way towards the town.

Sam lived with his wife, Blodwen, and their four children, Tessa, aged 13, David, 11, Richard, 7, and Sandra 14 months, in a neat, semi-detached house on a large estate. He was one of the 700 men to be made redundant in this latest cut. He had worked in the steel industry for nearly twenty years, ever since leaving school, and Madoc knew what a blow this would be for him.

As he turned into Sam's road Madoc spied his friend in the garden and he broke into a canter to catch him before he went inside again.

"Oh hello, Madoc," said Sam, as the big cat ran up to him and rubbed his face against Sam's leg. "Look, I've just found our first snowdrop. Hope the snow doesn't come and bury it. It's cold enough for anything. Come in the kitchen where it's nice and warm and have a saucer of milk."

"Purr, wurr," purred Madoc. He didn't make a habit of going inside people's houses – all those clean floors and the soft furniture made him uneasy – but Sam's was an exception. He liked his wife and the children too and their dog Miss Kip was a firm friend. He wasn't so keen on their two cats, Fritzy and Fred – typical stuck-up pets, in his opinion – but he'd never let on to Sam.

As Sam opened the door Miss Kip, who was golden in colour except for a black muzzle, black eyebrows and whiskers and a white patch on her chest, ran to greet Madoc, her tail wagging. Her silky ears were pricked forward and her big, brown eyes shone a welcome. She had one of the loveliest faces you can imagine, gentle like a fawn, intelligent and expressive. Under her shiny coat rippled powerful muscles.

Mrs Sam, as Madoc called her, was busy at the grill making toast.

"Hello, Madoc, nice to see you again," she said. "Come and sit by the fire and warm your paws."

Tessa, David and Richard, their mouths full of rice crispies, said something cheerful but incomprehensible and baby Sandra banged her spoon on her plastic bib.

But Fritzy and Fred, the cats, who had been sitting by the fire and resented Mrs Sam's invitation to Madoc to join them, both got up, put their tails in the air and stalked towards the door without so much as a miaow of welcome.

"Oh, all right, off you go you two and come back with some nice, fat mice," said Sam, opening the door for the two cats. "But mind you don't stay out long. It's very cold."

'Cold! Fleas!' thought Madoc with disdain. 'And as for catching any mice, a fine chance they've got. They'd be lucky to catch a lame robin with a suicide wish, those two. Pampered parasites!' But he didn't tell Sam what he thought.

"Well now, Madoc, what can we do for you?" asked Sam when Madoc had finished the saucer of warm milk Mrs Sam had given him.

Madoc began to tell him about the plan they had devised to find new work for the redundant cats.

"I know it's hard on you, Sam, and all the other humans," said Madoc, "but at least you'll get something to live on. We'll have nothing except the rats and mice we can catch and an animal, as you know, cannot live by mice alone. The Prime Minister is said to be a cat lover so I'm sure she'll understand and find us jobs."

Since the mid-1970s women prime ministers had been the fashion and this one was a woman.

"Well, I wouldn't be too sure of that, my friend," said Sam, not wishing to dampen his enthusiasm but at the same time not wanting to raise his hopes too high. "She's got an awful lot on her plate at the moment, you know. Six million unemployed, the colonisation of Mars, the Eskimo invasion of the Orkneys, to

8

name but a few problems. However, what's my role in all this?"

"Well, I thought," said Madoc, giving his fur a quick lick. It's something cats often do when they are about to seek a favour. They remember that advice learned at their mother's paw: 'When in Doubt, Lick'. "I thought," he continued, "that you and your friends might be able to look after the kittens and mother cats who'll be unable to march with us. We've got quite a few expecting kittens now and obviously they can't do the long journey to London and they'll need food and milk."

"Oh, let me look after them," begged Tessa. "I'd love to do that and my friends at school would help."

"If you ask Owain Butcher nicely I'm sure he'll give you a few scraps," added her mother. "Now hurry up all of you or you'll be late for school."

"I'll make you some boots like Puss in Boots in my leatherwork class," volunteered David.

"And I'll draw you a map showing all the mountains and rivers," added Richard, "so you know where to go and don't get drowned or anything."

"*Diolch yn fawr*," purred Madoc, "that'll be most useful."

Baby Sandra still couldn't talk properly but Madoc knew from her gurgles and her banging spoon that she, too, wished him luck.

"Right, school, you three," interrupted Mrs Sam, holding out three coats and three mufflers. "You can go on talking about this when you get home this afternoon."

The two elder children ran ahead to catch their bus and Mrs Sam walked hand in hand with Richard to his school that was only a few hundred yards up the road.

Left alone, Madoc turned to his friend Sam.

"Could you help with transport? It'd take us months to get to London by paw and if you and some of your friends could give us lifts to Primrose Hill, our rallying spot, we'd be tremendously grateful, a million purrs we would."

"Well, I was going to sell the van, being out of work and all that," said Sam, "but I'll keep it now until we've got you lot sorted out. And I'll tell my mates and see what they can organise. Jack's a guard with British Rail so I'm sure he'd give a pile of you a ride in his guard's van, unofficial like."

"Quite so," said Madoc. "*Chwarae teg.* Fair play."

"*Chwarae teg*," echoed Sam.

"Just one more thing . . ." Madoc's big amber eyes were wide and appealing. "Could Miss Kip come with us? It'd make all the difference to have a big, strong dog with a fast turn of paw."

"Woof," said Miss Kip. "Woof, please, woof."

"Oh, very well," said Sam reluctantly. "But mind you be careful. No rushing across busy roads after rabbits. Remember the Green Cross Code the kids taught you."

"Woof," said Miss Kip, "woof, I will," and wagged her tail.

"Oh, thank you, purr, double purr. *Diolch yn fawr iawn*," said Madoc. "– Any chance of another small saucer before I go?"

CHAPTER FOUR

DURING the next month the cats' plans were finalised. Madoc set Rallying Day for March 21st, the first day of Spring, and, through the underdogs, advised groups of cats all over the country to meet on Primrose Hill the day before.

It was decided that for their journey to London the cats should separate, Madoc, Snowy Tom, Esmeralda the Efficient and Geraint the Growler travelling by train in the guard's van with the majority of the animals and the others, mainly the younger cats and kittens who were thought to be unruly and who, Madoc said, might cause an affray, going in Sam's van with Patchwork, Katie Cat, Rufus the Ratcatcher, Carlo and his caterwaulers and Miss Kip.

Jack the guard, Sam's friend, told them to be there for the early train which he was in charge of and on which there would be no changes. The three children, Tessa, David and Richard, volunteered to get up and escort the party to the station before school.

The postman, milkman and cleaning ladies on their way to work early were surprised to see so many cats of all colours, shapes and sizes walking together with such purpose.

"What are you, the Pied Piper of Hamelin?" joked the milkman to David who was leading the band. "Here, have a couple of pints, you'll need them."

"*Duw*, I thought I was dreaming," said Mrs Jones to Rose as she got out her mops to clean the college before the lecturers and students arrived. "You'd not find that many cats in a creamery. Scruffy lot, though, not a bit like our Marmaduke. Sixteen on his last birthday and fur as soft and silky as when he was a kitten."

And Mr Stamp, the postman, when he got back to his depot

was teased by his colleagues for imagining things. He was given, anyway, to writing poetry and people regarded him as a bit of a dreamer.

"Stampy's had another of his visions," laughed one man.

"I certainly have not," retorted Mr Stamp indignantly. "They was there. Saw them with me own eyes. Led by a boy about twelve and a huge, big black cat with a white waistcoat and enormous whiskers. Never seen anything like it in all me days on the road."

"Good luck," called Debbie, on her newspaper round. She was at school with Tessa and David and knew all about the expedition. "Safe journey and whiskers up!"

Obedient to the command, all the cats immediately raised their whiskers and striding out, with tails erect, they were soon at the station.

As the great, long inter-city train slowed down Madoc looked round anxiously for Jack. How awful, he thought, if he'd changed his mind or got a cold or something.

But he need not have worried. There was Jack waving at them from his van.

"Right, animals, best paws forward. Run!"

And with that every cat – even portly Snowy Tom – squeezed through the railings and ran for the train. At the rear Esmeralda the Efficient rounded up stragglers.

Within seconds the train was off. The children waved till Madoc's white nose, peeping out of the window, was lost to sight. "Good luck! See you soon!" they called.

"All safely aboard," said Tessa, who had been at the end of the procession with Esmeralda. "I do hope things work out well for them."

"Dad will be leaving with Miss Kip and the next lot soon," said David. "We'd better hurry back so we don't miss them."

"I'm hungry," said Richard, and they all realised they hadn't yet had their breakfast.

Working in steel as they did, the cats were used to noise but none had ever been on a train before. Madoc had quite a job calming them down and quietening their excited mews.

"Mousers!" he said in as loud a growl as he dared. "Quiet

please. We mustn't attract attention to ourselves. We're here as a special favour from Jack and if we start caterwauling and mewing there'll be complaints. So take a calm lick of your fur – we ought to look smart for the big city – and then settle down for a peaceful cat-nap. Remember, there are busy days ahead."

The train had gone so fast that soon they *were* approaching a great city.

"We're here, we're here," miaowed Silky Sarah, one of Madoc's kittens, with excitement. "It's London. I can see the Tower of London." She was a very well-informed animal.

"Sorry, Sarah," said Jack sympathetically, "it's not London, it's Chester. Still a long way to go."

"It would be," grumbled Geraint the Growler. "Can't stand much more of this."

"That tower is part of the city walls," continued Jack. "The Romans built those walls round the town originally, though the ones you see now were built about fifteen centuries later, on top, as it were."

"And what's that?" asked Felix, a small tortoiseshell, "with all that grass and a track and seats going high up in the air?"

"Oh, that's the racecourse," said Jack.

"Where Miss Kip races?" chorused the cats. They knew all about greyhounds.

"No, horses," said Jack. "Quite famous, actually. Come myself to every May meeting and win a bob or two." He paused. "Most parts, any road," he added, not wishing to tell lies.

After Chester the train gathered speed again and before long, out of the window on their left, the cats saw a canal lined with brightly painted boats and barges. On some, people were sitting out with mugs of coffee and rolls enjoying the morning sun. On one a black cat stretched itself lazily and ambled towards a saucer a young woman had put down for it.

"Now that," said Snowy Tom, licking his lips, "is the life. A bargee cat. A snug little cabin and regular meals served by adoring humans, a place on deck to lie in the sun and only a small area to patrol. A canal cat is a comfortable cat." And he began to purr wistfully.

"Oh, Snowy, you'd have to clean yourself up a bit first," said Felix. "No one would want you in a cabin with dirty paws and smelly fur."

But Snowy took no notice. His blue eyes had gone misty and his purrs came in little spurts. He was oblivious to all, thinking of warmth and comfort and good meals, perhaps with a saucer of port wine to follow and a slice of mature, creamy Stilton cheese.

After leaving the canal the train travelled between narrow banks covered in yellow primroses. Out in the open again the cats could see massive roadworks, with trucks and bulldozers and lots of men in orange and yellow jackets and tin hats working.

"They're making a motorway," said Madoc knowledgeably. He knew about these things from listening to the men at work and reading their newspapers.

The train sped on through green and open country where cows and sheep grazed. Many lambs had been born in the last few weeks and the cats could see them frolicking and gambolling in the fields, which gave them itchy paws. They wanted to be out there too in the spring sunshine, not cooped up in a stuffy train. At the sight of so much freedom miaows of discontent started, led, of course, by Geraint the Growler, and soon the noise had reached a crescendo of catcalls.

Knock, Knock! Bang! Rat-a-tat-tat! There was a loud knock on the door of the guard's van.

"Inspector Wheels. What's going on in there?"

"Right, vanish, all of you," said Jack. "It's the Inspector. Coming, sir!"

Jack opened the door to the Inspector.

"Anything wrong, Jack? Thought I heard an awful squeaking sound."

"Nothing to bother about, sir. Just adjusting this window. Needs a bit of oil."

"Needs a lot of oil from the din, I would say," said Inspector Wheels. "What's that in the corner?"

"That?" said Jack innocently, looking at the huddled lump of fur that had assembled itself in the corner of his van. "Oh, that's some old rug a traveller's taking to London. Thought it might take up too much room in a carriage so I put it in here for him."

"Can't think what anyone would want with a mangy rug like that," said the Inspector, "but very well, carry on."

"Thank you, sir," said Jack.

But the ordeal was not over.

"What in heaven's name's that?" Inspector Wheels' eye had been caught by the sight of Esmeralda who, though called the Efficient, was often more efficient at organising others than herself. She had been so busy seeing the cats into their 'rug formation' – which they had planned in case of emergency – that she had forgotten to join them. Now she sat, one paw raised, emerald eyes staring, whiskers still as stone.

The Inspector stepped a pace nearer, peering through his bi-focal spectacles.

"Oh, yes, a statue I picked up at a flea market," explained Jack hastily. He hated lying, but what else could he do? Madoc shuddered in his 'mat' at the word 'flea'. "Not worth much," added Jack, "but I like it. Keep it by me for a mascot."

"Well, all right, but don't bring it with you again. Takes up valuable space in the van."

"Very well, sir," said Jack, and he closed the door behind the Inspector.

"My goodness, that was a narrow squeak," said Madoc, stretching himself. It had been uncomfortable for the cats pretending to be a rug. They had had to curl themselves up so that only their backs showed – no faces, no whiskers, no paws. "Hope we don't have to do that again."

Then, turning to Esmeralda, he said sternly: "You foolish cat! With your inefficiency you nearly ruined everything. Thank goodness the Inspector didn't look any closer."

"Sorry, Madoc," said Esmeralda, whiskers drooping, tail between her legs, "I was only trying to make sure every animal's tail was tucked in and then . . ."

"Oh well, never mind," said Madoc. "How about a story to help us pass the time?"

"Oh yes," said Esmeralda, happy again. "I've got just the

15

thing for a long journey."

And as she purred her story the cats sat round, quiet, if you'll forgive the expression, as mice, ears pricked to hear every word.

She was just finishing when Madoc realised one of their number was missing. Snowy Tom was nowhere to be seen.

"Snowy Tom," he miaowed when the story was over, "where are you?"

But there was no answering miaow.

"What's happened to him? Surely he can't have fallen out of the window looking at those lambs?" said Madoc.

"Probably imagining them roast with new potatoes and mint sauce if I know him," observed Esmeralda. "Thinks of nothing but his creature comforts, that animal."

"And he'd *need* to think of them in this uncomfortable van," said Geraint the Growler ungratefully.

"Perhaps he went out with Jack," suggested Felix, "while we were listening to our story."

"He was certainly here when we were being a rug," said Silky Sarah. "I should know. I was unlucky enough to curl up next to him and the smell nearly finished me off. He really is revolting. I can't imagine why he was ever called Snowy."

"I suppose he was Snowy once when he was a kitten," said Felix, who liked to be fair and always give another animal the benefit of the doubt.

"Yes, he was supposed to have been a beautiful kitten," said Madoc. "At least that's what his mother said."

"Every kitten is beautiful in the eyes of its mother," remarked Esmeralda drily. "But this isn't getting us anywhere. Where *is* he? We must find him. It's not orderly to have a missing cat."

"Quite right, Esmeralda," said Madoc. "You're the efficient one, so you go and look for him. As Felix said, he must have gone out with Jack when no one was looking. But be careful and don't take any risks."

"Miaow," said Esmeralda, and with a quick lick of her fur she stationed herself by the door so that she could slip out quickly between Jack's legs when he opened it, which wasn't very long.

Esmeralda moved cautiously along the train which

fortunately wasn't too crowded. If it had been a train with corridors it might have been easier for her. But this smart inter-city had big open carriages, separated by sliding doors, and at every one she had to crouch under a seat and wait for a human being to open the door before she could get through.

She had just reached the First Class compartments when she heard a ticket collector.

"Tickets please, tickets please. Your ticket, madam."

"Mr Ticket Collector," said a fierce, high-pitched voice. "I have a complaint to make. This is an extremely smelly train. What are you going to do about it?"

"I agree, madam," answered the ticket collector, "there *is* a strange smell here, but the rest of the train is perfectly all right."

"Are you implying, my man," said the woman in even shriller tones, "that this disgusting, exceptionally pungent odour is something to do with me? I'll report you for insolence."

"No, not at all, madam," replied the ticket collector, "but it is strange that I haven't smelt it anywhere else. What have you got in that shopping bag? Perhaps something's gone off."

"Gone off! Gone off!" echoed the woman indignantly. "I never buy anything but the best. And I've paid for a first-class seat. I'll not stand for any more of this. Pull the alarm and call me a taxi."

"Madam," pursued the ticket collector with the utmost patience, "we are in the middle of nowhere. I couldn't get you a taxi here if I tried. I believe the offensive odour to which you refer is coming from this hat on the seat next to you. I have been commended before for my excellent sense of smell and my nose tells me that the culprit lies here, in your head attire. Is it, perhaps, skunk?"

"This is intolerable!" expostulated the woman. "First you insult me and now you say my expensive mink hat, purchased by my late husband, Sir Archibald Knowall, from the country's top furrier, is skunk. Read the label for yourself, you ignorant man, and tell me then if you think it's skunk. Look!"

Lady Knowall picked up the hat and let out a loud, piercing scream.

For out of the soft, upturned hat leapt an enormous, exceptionally scruffy, off-white tom cat, with bent whiskers and two torn ears.

"Quick, Snowy, here! Run!" miaowed Esmeralda urgently.

And Snowy followed her at full pelt, back through the carriages, where, by a stroke of luck, all the doors were open, to the guard's van.

"Miaow, miaow," she gasped, her breath coming fast, "let us in. It's me, Esmeralda, and Snowy. Miaow, miaow."

Jack opened the door. He was horrified when he heard what had happened and told Madoc he must keep his troupe in order or there'd be trouble.

"We're coming into Rugby now," he told them, "and after that it's non-stop to London, so try and behave yourselves. I'll go and see if I can sort something out with Lady Knowall."

The cats were subdued. Some washed their faces in embarrassment while others sat on their haunches staring into space, as if disclaiming all responsibility for the episode. Snowy

Tom slunk into the corner and curled up on some sacking.

For about half an hour there was not a sound in the guard's can. Madoc gave a low purr of relief. At least it would not be long now before they reached their destination.

But he'd purred too soon. Excited squeaks and growls came from the corner where Snowy lay on his sacking.

"I'll catch you by your whiskers," hissed Felix.

"Wait till I get my paws on you," growled Sarah.

"Nothing but trouble, you lot. I'll soon put an end to that," growled Geraint.

"Catch that mouse, catch that mouse!" chanted the other cats in unison.

"Quiet, you unruly animals!" commanded Madoc. "You know what Jack said. What's the matter?"

As he walked over the source of the excitement became plain. Snowy, in an effort to get more comfortable, had given an extra tug to the sacking he'd been lying on and pulled it off a cage, exposing, for all to see, a magnificent mouse-house, complete with ladders and wheels and toys – and six fat white mice.

"Stop it, this instant," said Madoc. "Can't you see these mice are someone's pets? Apologise immediately, all of you, or I'll send you home by the next train."

"Sorry, mice," said Felix. "I can see now you're not fair game. We shouldn't have frightened you."

"Sorry," said Sarah. "It was just instinct. We didn't mean it."

"Sorry," miaowed the other cats.

"I'm not," muttered Geraint the Growler, but Madoc ignored him.

By the time Jack returned all was quiet, but he couldn't help noticing that the sacking had fallen off the mouse-house.

"Well, what good animals you are," he said. "The sacking's fallen off the mouse-house and not one of you has raised a paw in anger."

"Purr," said Madoc.

"I didn't dare tell you the mice were there," continued Jack, "as I thought you'd try and get at them and frighten them to death and they belong to a little girl who loves them dearly. She couldn't take them with her in the carriage, you understand, as not everyone's too fond of mice."

"And they smell," added Snowy, who was hardly one to criticise.

"Well, yes, exactly," said Jack. "Which brings me to Lady Knowall. We've said we'll refund her fare and she's agreed to drop the matter of Snowy Tom."

"Thank goodness for that," said Madoc with a sigh of relief. "I was really worried you and the ticket collector might get into trouble."

"Yes, indeed," agreed Jack. He was fond of the cats but he'd be glad when this particular journey was over.

"Now we're approaching London," he told them, "so be prepared to jump out quickly. The train goes through Primrose Hill and I've arranged to stop it for a couple of minutes there so you can make a dash for it. My sister's cat, Conrad, who lives near here and knows the territory, will meet you and take you to your rendezvous. It'll be a lot easier than going through the ticket barrier at Euston. So goodbye for now and best of luck."

"Thank you, Jack, for all your help," said Madoc, extending a paw. "We're most grateful. Now, all cats line up and prepare to jump!"

"We are now approaching Euston," said a voice on the intercom. "Your train is on time. We hope you have had a pleasant journey. Remember to take all your baggage with you when you leave the train. Thank you."

No sooner had the voice finished its announcement than the train slowed down and came to a halt. Jack opened the door.

"Every cat out! Run!"

Quick as paws could, the cats, led by Madoc, with Esmeralda the Efficient in the rear, ran across the railway lines towards the road beyond.

On the train the announcer's voice said: "Your train is now two minutes late. We apologise for any inconvenience this may cause. The delay is due to an unforeseen circumstance."

"There're an awful lot of railway lines," panted Snowy Tom, jumping over yet another set of rails. "I wish I hadn't stolen that chicken from the restaurant car."

"You perfectly appalling animal," Esmeralda rebuked him. "Don't you ever think of anyone else but yourself?"

"Not really," said Snowy.

"Quick," warned Esmeralda, "a train's coming! We don't want to get run over."

The cats just cleared the line as another express thundered through, this time on its way north.

"Miaow, cats, over here! It's me, Conrad!" A handsome, corn-coloured cat was calling from a garden that backed onto the railway line. "Follow me!"

"Nice to meet you, Conrad," said Madoc. "Good of you to help."

"Mousers of the world, unite!" miaowed Conrad with fervour. "We cats must stick together. Come on, it's not all that far."

"There seem to be a lot of houses and streets here," remarked Madoc, puzzled. "I thought Primrose Hill was, well, a green hill covered in primroses."

"Well, it's a hill and there's grass," said Conrad, "and I'm sure you'll be very comfortable there – a few bushes and so on to shelter under if the temperature drops. You know what these cold March nights can be like. Even the first day of Spring isn't always very springlike. I won't join you, if you don't mind. Molly, Jack's sister you know, doesn't like me out at night. Gets lonely, you understand."

Odd, these domestic cats, thought Madoc, to want to stay indoors when you could be out on the tiles – but all he said was "Quite."

After what seemed to the country cats an eternity of noise, traffic and crowded street, they reached the open park that is Primrose Hill.

"I'll leave you now," said Conrad. "Must get back for my lunch. Molly's expecting me. See you around."

"So long, Conrad, and thanks," purred Madoc. "Now cats," he continued, turning to his band, "I suggest we investigate a few dustbins, do a bit of mousing and settle down and wait for the others. At least there's plenty of grass here. Remember to have a good chew at that; it's good for the digestion."

As the afternoon progressed more and more cats arrived – from the Midlands, from Tyneside, from Cumbria, from South Wales and, last of all, just as dusk was falling, the contingent from Scotland, the Gallant 99 led by Hamish McPurr, an enormous tabby with yellow eyes and a kink in his tail. He had caught it in a trap when he was a kitten and it never recovered.

Sam's van, with Patchwork, Carlo and the Caterwaulers, Katie Cat, Rufus the Ratcatcher, Miss Kip and a pile of young cats and kittens, had drawn up by the hill just as a nearby church clock was striking four.

Madoc ran to rub his cheek against Sam's leg. "Good to see you," he said. "Have a good journey?"

"Yes, thanks," said Sam. "The old van stood up well to the motorway and the cats were pretty well behaved on the whole, though a bit noisy. Carlo would insist on caterwauling for almost the entire journey. Said he must get the marching song right for tomorrow. Can't say it's done my ears much good and after about 150 miles poor Miss Kip was driven into snapping at them – something she hardly ever does – she could stand it no longer. So at least the last few miles have been fairly restful."

"Oh dear," said Madoc, thankful, for all the dramas of the journey, that he had taken the train. "Did you stop anywhere?"

"Just one motorway café so they could stretch their paws, have a saucer of milk and do all the usual things. Some of the kittens were a bit unruly then and Katie Cat had to speak to them severelyy then and Katie Cat had to speak to them severely – you know how sensible she is, being a partly domesticated cat and all that – but no disasters.

"Oh and Rufus caught three rats and took them to the Motorway Services Manager. He seemed very impressed and said he'd take him on his staff any time. How about you?"

"Well, there were incidents," answered Madoc with a low growl, "but we're all here in one piece, that's the main thing. What are your plans?"

"I'll turn round and go home now," said Sam, "and I'll come back with the children just as soon as I can. They've got a couple of days holiday from school this week and can't bear to miss all the excitement. Their mother says she'll look after your kittens, by the way, with Tessa's friend Debbie."

"Purr," said Madoc.

"Fritzy and Fred, the cats, didn't seem interested though," he added.

'I'll bet they didn't, lazy bundles of overweight fur and pampered whiskers,' thought Madoc, but all he said was "Well, goodbye Sam, and thanks again."

"Goodbye Madoc, Patchwork, Katie Cat; see you soon. And goodbye Miss Kip," he added, patting his dog's head. "Keep an eye on these cats and be careful yourself. You know we think you're the best hound in the world."

"Bark," said Kip, and jumped up to lick his face.

"Miaow," said the cats. "Goodbye."

CHAPTER FIVE

THE underdogs had done a good job spreading the word around the country and when Madoc counted heads that evening he found that over five thousand cats had assembled on Primrose Hill to prepare for their march on Downing Street the following day.

That night the residents of that quiet London borough were puzzled by the strange noises that seemed to be coming from their hill. One young woman looked out of her flat window and thought she saw the hill moving as if an army of moles had taken it over. And a man coming back from work in the City, taking his usual route home from the underground station across the hill, thought space invaders had landed and phoned the police.

"Yes, sir, we'll investigate," said the sergeant at the station. But he didn't attach much importance to the report.

"Another crackpot," he told his constable. "I wish the Press wouldn't make so much fuss about these UFO sightings. An article on UFOs in the Sunday papers and the next day we're inundated with calls. Only wish the public were as good at reporting real crimes."

"Hope it's not the start of another sit-out by those loonies from the End of the World Society," said the constable. "They made a right mess of the hill last year with their banners and altars and Tablets of the Lord."

"Oh, we're safe enough at the moment," chuckled the sergeant. "They make quite sure the end of the world only comes in the summer. Much too cold for a sit-out at this time of year, even if it is nearly the first day of Spring. All the same, Constable, better pop up and have a look. Can never be too careful these days."

"Yes, sir. Very good, sir," and PC John Friar, known in the Force as Tuck because of his wide girth, checked that his pencil was sharpened and that his notebook had not run out of pages and went on his way to investigate.

With him went PC Titch Williams, the shortest constable in the Force, for, as you know, policemen these days go everywhere in twos.

Little did they know it, but Tuck and Titch were about to crack one of the greatest crime rackets of the decade.

CHAPTER SIX

"FIVE thousand, I reckon," said the man in the dirty rain-coat and Al Capone style hat.

"Five thousand, eh?" echoed Slimey Jim, stubbing out a cigarette in the already overflowing saucer that stood next to three dirty mugs and a screwed up chip paper on the cluttered trestle table before him. "Five thousand. So if we reckon £5 each cat, that's er, that's, nought times five is, er, is er, nought and, er, nought times five is . . ."

"Twenty-five grand," interrupted Al Capone, which is what John Smith preferred to be called.

"Twenty-five thousand?" murmured Slimey Jim, relieved someone else had done the sum and spared him the embarrassment of getting it wrong. "Not bad for a night's work, eh? Think you can manage it?"

"No trouble," said Bert, a big, muscular man who favoured the woolly cap as winter headgear. "No trouble."

"Fred and Harry'll give us a hand," said Al Capone. "And Sid'll drive the pantechnicon. They're all squared. Mum's the word. Should have the whole job sewn up by midnight, no messing. Customers all sorted out for the skins, then?"

"Could take the same again," Slimey Jim told him, wiping his sweaty brow with his shirt sleeve. "However much these do-gooders protest, people still like the genuine article. This nylon rubbish isn't a patch on real, soft fur. Give me a nice, thick fur coat any day – and a hat and a pair of gloves to match. What do you say, Bert?"

"No trouble," answered Bert, whose vocabulary was limited. "No trouble."

"No there, for once, you're right, Bert. There are so many damn cats around these days, a hundred here, a thousand

there, will not be missed. And you'd be amazed the way the skins make up into such fashionable garments. Wife had one the other day and you couldn't tell it from mink.

"Mind you," continued Slimey, "you need nice, fresh fur. Mustn't leave the dead bodies lying around too long in their smart fur coats, eh, Capone?"

"No, boss."

"No, indeed," confirmed Slimey, who gloried in the title of Director General of Catskins Ltd, a business he had founded himself. "No. Whip the skins off their little furry backs before you can say whiskers, clean them up, hang them nice and neat in our special drying room and in no time at all we've got a very marketable product. Stroke of genius, I reckon. Pay nothing for our raw material and, as far as I can see, the supply is endless. Just need a few skilful operators to catch the little beasts and a nice touch with the skinning later and Bob's your uncle, eh, Capone, eh?"

"Quite right, boss. Sure was a brilliant idea. And what's the world want with all them cats, anyway? Be a better place without them. You might say we're performing a useful service."

"You might indeed," said Slimey. "And making ourselves a nice few bob in the process."

"No trouble," said Bert.

"Smart chap, Bert," said Slimey, "'cos here's what I want to know. No chance of those pals of yours, Fred and who was it?"

"Harry," supplied Al Capone.

"Fred and Harry going all sentimental on us and falling down on the job, I hope? We want all five thousand of them cats brought back here tonight and skinned and ready for the rag trade by the morning."

"As I said, I've squared them," said Al Capone irritably. "Once we've got the cats in the lorry we'll come straight back here and start on the skinning job. Fred and Harry'll make their own way and me an' Bert an' Sid'll come in the lorry having done the necessary."

"No trouble," said Bert, taking off his once white woolly hat with the bobble and wringing it in his mittened hands. "No trouble."

"I don't want you killing them, you idiot," warned Slimey, who didn't care for Bert's action with the hat. "That's got to be done here by the proper method. Can't risk getting their fur messed up, not good for business, see. Every cat's got to be delivered here alive. For every one that isn't I deduct so much from your wages, get it?"

"No trouble," said Bert.

"OK, boss, leave it to us, we're the experts," said Al Capone, and he adjusted the red paper carnation in the wide lapel of his 1930s style suit. "Shouldn't take more than an hour to get back here in the middle of the night, even with Sid at the wheel, so see you later."

"No trouble," said Bert, pulling the woolly hat back on his head and nodding with such vigour it nearly fell off.

"You'll lose that bobble one day," said Slimey Jim. "Why don't you get it sewn on firmly?"

"No trouble," answered Bert.

"Oh, get along with you," said Slimey. "And no mistakes, mind you. I've got valuable customers waiting for them pelts and I've got the reputation of Catskins Ltd to think of."

A lorry was parked in the driveway of the big, isolated house and at its wheel sat Sid. He was busy sending messages on his Citizen's Band radio and was rather annoyed when Al Capone and Bert interrupted him.

"Hello, Blue Moon, this is Saucer Eyes. Eyeball at Big C . . ." he was saying.

"Oh, come on, pack it in, we've got work to do," said Al Capone, jumping in and switching off the set.

"Oh all right," said Sid. "But be careful with my gear. That cost a lot of money, you know."

There was no sign or board outside Pinewood House to indicate it was the headquarters of Catskins Ltd because, of course, the whole operation was strictly illegal. And Sid's lorry bore no lettering. He had the usual number plates at the front and back but even these were not that usual as he changed them whenever he thought necessary to avoid the Law.

"Come on," said Al Capone, making room for Bert next to him in the front of the lorry, "let's get on with it."

"Right," said Sid, revving the powerful engine. "Sooner out, sooner back."

"No trouble," said Bert.

CHAPTER SEVEN

CATS often like to prowl about at night and take their rest in the day, but on this night Madoc ordered cat-naps for all so they would be fresh for the march in the morning.

Good as gold, they had all settled down, some snoring peacefully, others jerking their paws and twitching their noses in rat-catching dreams, when four dark figures in masks emerged from a pantechnicon parked at the side of the hill. Two carried big canisters fitted with nozzle sprays and the other two had nets.

"Right," whispered Al Capone, "as soon as me and Bert starts spraying, you, Harry, and you, Fred, come up behind with those nets and catch as many of the nasty little furry things as you can. Then straight back to the lorry and throw them in. But, mind you, don't get too rough. We don't want any of the flea-ridden creatures dying on us yet – it affects the quality of their fur.

"So fling them in and straight back for another load, see? We wants the hill cleared and five thousand miserable moggies packed in that lorry by 2 a.m. at the latest. See? No messing. Then you can scarper. Slimey'll fix you up with your share of the dough back at HQ Right?"

"Not right," said Harry, a beanpole of a man in tight blue jeans and a navy duffle coat with mask to match. "We want the readies now, see. No brown uns, blue uns and greens uns, no job, and that's final."

"Yeah," added Fred, who was missing a front tooth and had a safety pin dangling from his left ear. "No dough, no cats. 'alf now an' 'alf when the cats are in the bag, so to speak. That's fair."

"No trouble," said Bert.

"Oh shut up, you," snapped Al Capone. "Oh very well," he added, turning to Harry and Fred. Time was getting on and he couldn't afford to stand there arguing all night. "Here you are." And he shoved a wad of notes into each man's mittened hand. "And mind you catch every one."

"No trouble," added Bert, and he nodded so hard the bobble fell off his hat, but no one noticed.

"Can't you ever say anything else?" Al Capone turned on his partner in crime. He was in a fair rage now. His plan to doublecross Harry and Fred had failed and in the bitter cold of this March night he was rapidly going off the whole idea of cat-snatching as a way of earning a living.

"No trouble," mumbled Bert under his breath, and the sound came as near to swearing as Bert could manage.

"Right," said Al Capone, "have you got your cat gas switched on?"

"No trouble," affirmed Bert.

"Action!"

The two men ran across the grass towards the sleeping cats, closely followed by Harry and Fred with their nets. The gas paralysed the animals and when Fred and Harry started to bundle them into their nets they found they couldn't fight back. Their paws wouldn't move and try as hard as they could they were not able to unsheath their claws to scratch. They couldn't even miaow a warning to their friends.

As Al Capone and Bert continued to pump the hateful gas Fred and Harry dragged their full nets back to the waiting pantechnicon to dump their load.

At the same moment a panda car containing Police Constables Friar and Williams drew up on the opposite side of the hill.

"Something funny going on over there," said PC Titch Williams, who was the passenger and was known for the length of his sight as well as for the shortness of his stature. "Thought I saw a couple of blokes dragging something towards that lorry over there. Look, they've got the back down and they're throwing things in."

"Can't see a thing," said PC Friar Tuck, "but I'll take your word for it. Let's investigate."

The two constables jumped out of the car and ran across the hill towards the spot where Titch had seen the action.

"Good God, cats, hundreds of them!" exclaimed Titch. "And two men with watering cans!"

"They're not watering cans, they're bombs," said Tuck. "Hurry!" And he blew a long, piercing note on his whistle.

It didn't attract any more policemen to the scene but it did have the effect of waking all the cats who had not yet been bagged and their faithful friend Miss Kip, the golden greyhound.

"The Fuzz!" shouted Al Capone. "Scarper. We've been shopped. Scarper!"

"No trouble," choked Bert, and dropping their cat gas canisters the two men ran hell for leather for the pantechnicon.

"Scarper!" shouted Al Capone to Fred and Harry as they turned back from the lorry with their nets to collect another load. "Scarper!"

Fred and Harry didn't need telling twice. At the first indication of trouble they were off down the hill like a couple of Olympic sprinters.

Bundling the nets in with the cats, Al Capone fastened the lorry door and raced to the front with Bert at his heels.

"Depot One as fast as you can. The secret route," Al Capone ordered Sid, who already had the engine running.

"JEY 23 . . . missed it, confound it," exclaimed an out-of-breath PC Titch, who had strained his eyes to the utmost to catch the lorry's numberplate in the light from the street lamps.

But he needn't have worried. Faster almost than sound, a golden greyhound had sped across the hill and was now trailing the lorry at a speed of some 40 m.p.h. as it made its way north out of the big city.

"Got it, Titch?" asked PC Tuck, panting up behind his more agile friend.

"Couldn't quite get the end but it's JEY 23 something so at least we've got a bit to go on," answered Titch.

"But what on earth were they doing," mused Tuck, "all alone on this hill with a pile of cats?"

"May I be of assistance?" It was Madoc speaking. "Only I think I've found some evidence."

"What d'you say, Titch?" asked Tuck. "Have you shrunk or something?" He realised the voice came from some way below him but he didn't think even Titch was that small.

"I didn't say anything," answered Titch. "Is this place haunted or something?"

"Purr, it's me," said Madoc, running his cheek against Tuck's big leg, enclosed in its rough serge policeman's uniform. "It's me, Madoc the Magnificent."

"Good God, *Duw*, it's one of them cats," exclaimed Titch, who also came from Wales and so spoke both Welsh and English, especially when agitated. "Yes certainly, Mr Cat, we'll need all the help we can get to solve this one."

"What's your evidence?" asked PC Tuck.

"This," answered Madoc, proferring a grubby woolly bobble that once might have been described as white. "It must be part of an article of clothing."

"Exhibit One," wrote Titch in his note-book, "bobble, woolly, dirty, one. Anything else to tell us, Mr Cat?"

"Yes," said Madoc, "they've cat-napped about a hundred of our colleagues. I think they must be in the fur trade. Unless we can catch them the poor animals will be fur coats and gloves before we can say kippers. If it hadn't been for you two brave constables we might all have perished. It's a golden rule with cats to have at least one on guard but tonight we made an exception and ordered cat-naps for all so we could be fresh for the morning."

"Why, what's happening in the morning?" asked Tuck, who was beginning to think the whole thing was a dream.

"We're marching on Downing Street with our petition," said Madoc. And he began to tell the constables all about their plans.

"Well, you'll need a police escort for that," said Titch. "Stands to reason, don't it? Everyone gets a police escort these days. Lucky we found you. But first you must come back with us to the Station and make a statement about this incident."

"And have a nice, warm saucer of milk," added Tuck, always conscious of the benefits of food and drink.

"All cats checked, sah! 4,901 animals present and correct, 99 missing, sah!" Hamish, the Purr of McPurrs, drew himself to his full height, which was considerable, and saluted Madoc, the acknowledged leader of the rally.

"Which group are they from, Hamish?" asked Madoc.

"Ma own clan, Madoc, sah!" replied the enormous tabby from Galashiels, who had taken a week to get down from Scotland with his followers. "Every one a McPurr. It's a terrible thing.We must get them back."

"We will, Hamish, we will," said Madoc, sounding more confident than he was. He knew from stories he had heard how quickly these fur pirates worked. "Since it's your animals that are missing you'd better come with me to the Station to make a statement. I expect they'll want detailed descriptions."

"Right," said Hamish, "I'm your cat."

"You, Patchwork," continued Madoc, turning to his second in command, "you take over here while I'm away and see the animals get a bit of shut-eye before the morning. I don't think the thieves will risk anything more tonight."

And, tails in the air, Hamish and Madoc the Magnificent followed the two constables back to the panda car.

As they drove to the Station Madoc explained how Miss Kip, the golden greyhound and the Fastest Paw in the West, had pursued the cat-nappers.

"She'll rescue your gang, I'm sure, Hamish," he reassured his Scottish friend. "And she won't let those criminals out of her sight either," he added, addressing the constables.

'I just hope she gets there in time,' he said to himself, and a shudder went through his fur as he thought of those poor cats, who had travelled all those hundreds of miles to promote their cause, being skinned and made into fur coats and gloves for uncaring humans.

CHAPTER EIGHT

HAMISH'S Gallant 99 were still missing when dawn broke over Primrose Hill on March the 21st, but the march had to go on.

"Right," said Madoc, "has every cat put his pawmark to the petition? What about that bunch of kittens over there? Can you check, Sergeant Growler, that they've pawmarked? Wouldn't want to leave anyone out."

"Yes, sir," said Sergeant Growler, raising a paw in salute. Then, turning, he went at a brisk, military trot towards the kittens who appeared to be playing cat and mouse with an old potato that must have dropped out of someone's shopping bag.

"Come on now, you 'orrible little kittens you," roared Sergeant Growler. He was a real sergeant-major of a cat. Even his whiskers had been trained over the years to cling together so they looked more like a moustache. "'ave you pawmarked?"

"No," mewed one mischievous-looking tabby, "we didn't know we had to. Can't we finish our game first?"

"No, you most certainly cannot, you 'orrible load of moth-eaten fur. Right, all of you, into line, sharpish. One, two, one, two . . ." And Sergeant Growler marched them all off to Patchwork who was in charge of pawmarking operations.

The sun was climbing in the sky and beginning to warm the cold earth. It had been a long winter but now it was going to be a lovely spring day. Some daffodils that had been just buds the day before had burst into flower with the promise of warmth and their golden raiment brightened the bare hill, giving new heart to the cats, still worried about the events of the preceding night.

Detaching himself from the crowd, Madoc jumped up onto the branch of a tree and began to address his followers.

"Friends and fellow mousers," he said. "Group yourselves into your regional sections, wave your banners high and follow me! And as we march let us sing our rallying song:

> "Steel Town Cats we'll fight like tigers,
> Sabre-toothed and claws well sharpened,
> Spit and scratch and snarl and bite
> And we shall win the day!"

Still singing, Madoc the Magnificent, mouser supreme, leapt down and, paw before determined paw, led his worker cats down Primrose Hill and across the busy road to Regent's Park. Flanking them, as escort, marched Police Constables Tuck and Titch.

Regent's Park is famous for its zoo and as the cats marched past the high enclosure all the animals joined in the song:

> "For we are the mousers," roared the lions.
> "Mousers bold are we," growled the tigers.
> "Stretch your paws, extend your claws,
> And raise your hackles high!"

Then the elephants trumpeted:

> "We shall show them we mean business,
> They will ask whatever is this?"

And the monkeys finished off in high-pitched chatter:

> "March with us, oh brave young purrcats
> And we shall win the day!"

Through Regent's Park, down Baker Street, up Oxford Street to the Circus, down Regent's Street the procession marched. Traffic was brought to a standstill and shoppers exclaimed in disbelief as the furry band made its relentless way towards the Seat of Power.

"Quite right, too!" shouted a man who had climbed the Eros statue in Piccadilly Circus to get a better view of the proceedings. The hoardings that had been up for so long had just been taken away. "Jobs for mousers, I say. The place is over-run with vermin. Go to it, cats!"

By the time the cats reached Trafalgar Square all the reporters had come down from Fleet Street, even from as far as Wapping, to write about the event for their newspapers. As the procession swirled round the bottom of the square into

37

Whitehall the stone lions that guard Nelson's Column got up onto their hind legs and roared approval.

When the reporter from the *Daily Mail* put this in his story he was told off by his news editor for letting his imagination run wild.

"You've been drinking," the news editor said.

But he hadn't. It was all quite true.

Even the pigeons that fly in their thousands round the square gave grudging approval to the cats and chirped in with part of

the chorus.

"At least," said Polly Pigeon to her friend Pamela, "if they're ratting and mousing they'll leave us alone. Always remember the sad fate of my first mate, Percy. Caught by an alley cat while basking in the sun after a nice bath. Ate every bit of him except his beak. Hope the miserable moggie died of indigestion. He was a tough old bird at any rate, old Perce. Must have caused a twinge or two."

"Eyes right!" roared Sergeant Growler as they went past

Horse Guards and, once again, he gave the salute.

"Right turn!" he ordered as the procession approached Downing Street.

Still singing, in rather hoarse miaows by this time it must be admitted, the cats lined up outside Number 10. As you know, people are no longer allowed beyond a certain point in the street unless they have special passes but up till now there's been no ruling on cats, so there seemed no reason for the policeman on duty not to let them past the barriers.

Boldly Madoc and Hamish McPurr, who had the petition strapped to his back, stepped forward and addressed the policeman guarding the door.

"Petition for the PM, is it?" asked the duty constable. "Get a lot of those these days. Anything special?"

"Yes, it's very special," said Madoc. "Hundreds of worker cats all over the country have been made redundant because of the closing of steel works and other factories and we're here to demand work. We're all top-rate mousers."

"There's nothing new in that," said the constable. "Last week it was the school leavers, the week before that the over fifties and before that the university graduates. Couldn't do a thing for any of them, she couldn't, so I don't know what chance you lot've got. Still, we'll ring the bell. Gives them something to do, eh?" And the constable gave a long peal on the bell.

After a few seconds the door opened and a tall, elegant man in a pin-striped suit and wearing rimless spectacles on the end of his nose peered out.

"Petition, sir," said the constable, " for the PM. Five thousand pawmarks, I understand."

"Oh, it's the felines, is it?" the pin-striped gentleman said, looking down his nose so much that his glasses nearly fell off. "The lowest order of the leonine species."

"Er, what's that?" queried the constable. "You mean you were born under the sign of Leo? I'm a Taurus myself. Today's horoscope told me to prepare for a surprise – well, I got that all right, didn't I?"

"Yes, quite so," said the superior gentleman, and turning

into the house he began calling "Augustus, come here, Augustus, Augustus!"

The next minute a highly superior cat appeared on the scene. With his black and white markings he was almost pin-striped himself and he looked down his nose at Madoc and his band just like the superior man – but he didn't wear spectacles.

"Augustus, you are to see to this. PM's instructions. She heard about this rabble on Breakfast Television. No need to waste too much time with them, I would think."

"Leave it to me, sir," said Augustus, and waved a dismissive paw. Then, drawing himself up to his full height, which was considerable, he turned to Madoc. "Well, my cat, what have you got for us today? I'm not sure you shouldn't have used the tradesmen's entrance." He brushed a snow-white paw across his nose and sniffed in disgust.

Indeed, looking at this elegant animal, with his glossy, beautifully-groomed coat and manicured claws, Madoc, Hamish, Patchwork, and their followers felt at a considerable disadvantage. Augustus was sleek and fat; they were mostly skinny and their fur was patchy. Most of the toms had torn ears from fighting and Patchwork had only half a nose, the rest having been ripped off in a bout with a rat. The females, though they did what they could to keep their coats smart, were generally too tired from a combination of heavy mousing duties and looking after large families of kittens to be able to devote a lot of time to grooming and their fur was dull. As for the kittens, a more disreputable looking bunch of ragamuffins would be hard to imagine.

However, Madoc had not come all the way from North Wales to be put off by a pin-striped cat.

"We've got a petition," he said. "We want the Prime Minister to give us work. As mousers and ratters there's none to beat us and we're willing to turn our paws to anything."

"All right," said Augustus, "paw it over and I'll see that she gets it. Don't expect too much, though. Modern poisons have made mousing and ratting a thing of the past – or perhaps you don't know about such modern technology in your part of the world?"

41

Before Madoc could reply to the insult Augustus had turned tail and gone back into the house.

"Pussy, wussy, wussy," they heard a woman's voice calling, "come and get your lunch before I go to the House. Lamb's liver for you today, you clever, handsome cat."

Lamb's liver! Madoc's mouth began to water. He'd only had it once when Sam brought him some as a special treat the time he'd won the Christmas raffle of a hamper. His eyes went misty and he began to purr gently.

"Don't know what you're sounding so cheerful about," said the constable. "Not much chance, I'd say. Though, mind you, he's quite wrong about poisons, that stuck-up Augustus. Vermin gets accustomed to them, they does, and the only ones that gets hurt are the children and dogs that go and eat them instead. Shouldn't think that mamby-pamby cat has ever caught a decent mouse in his life."

"What do we do now?" asked Madoc. "How do we know if she'll help us?"

"Hang about a bit," advised the constable. "She may decide to see you, you never know."

So Madoc and Hamish rejoined their colleagues and waited. Actually they were glad of a bit of a rest, being pawsore and weary from the long march, and the spring sunshine was pleasantly warm on their backs. They might even have started purring had they not been so worried about Hamish's missing Gallant 99 and brave Miss Kip.

CHAPTER NINE

⁂

THE lorry, carrying the ninety-nine unconscious cats, with Al Capone, Bert and Sid, the driver, squashed together on the front seat, soon reached the outskirts of the city. Miss Kip, the golden greyhound, was still in pursuit. Whatever happened she must not lose sight of the vehicle – ninety-nine cats' lives depended on that.

Suddenly the lorry swerved off the main road and turned into a yard. Al Capone jumped out.

"Quick, chop-chop, no time to waste," he said as two men ran out to meet them. "We want them number plates off and the lorry resprayed pink within half an hour, no messing."

"Not possible, guv," said one man. "Good three hours' work there. Can't be done."

"No such word as can't," said Al Capone sharply. "Here, will this make it worth your while?" And he handed them a fifty pound note.

"Right, guv, as you say."

The two men set to work, removing the number plates and replacing them with new ones. Then they started spraying with pink paint. Bert and Sid were still in the front seat.

"Close the window, you idiot," said Sid, "or we'll be pink as icing on a party cake."

"No trouble," said Bert, who had not uttered since their rush to get away from Primrose Hill.

"Not exactly talkative, are you?" said Sid. "Ever have a conversation?"

"No trouble," said Bert.

Meanwhile the cats, one by one, were coming to their senses. Gordon o' the Glens was the first to regain consciousness, followed by Angus McFisher and Wee Willie White Paws.

"What's happening?" asked Wee Willie nervously. The smell of paint was dreadful and it reminded him of the gas that had knocked them all unconscious on Primrose Hill just as they were settling down for the night.

"I'm not sure," said Gordon, a smoky grey animal, "but I think they must be respraying this vehicle we're in, changing its colour so it won't be recognised."

"And earlier, just as I was coming round," said Angus, bright ginger from the tip of his nose to the end of this tail, "I heard a sort of squeaking sound and a clatter of metal. I wonder what that could have been?"

"Bark, bark, bark!"

"Oh, listen," squealed Wee Willie, "a bark, and it sounds friendly."

"Bark, bark, it's me, Miss Kip, can you hear me?"

"Yes, Miss Kip, we can, we're here," miaowed Gordon in reply, "a bit woozy but otherwise OK."

"Now listen," barked Miss Kip urgently, "we haven't got much time. I've followed you all the way from Primrose Hill and I'll not lose sight of you, I promise. As soon as I can I'll rescue you. Keep your spirits up and don't worry."

"But how?" wailed Wee Willie. "We're lost, we're finished, oh miaow, miaow, miaow. I'll never again see the bonnie, bonnie banks o' Loch Lomond. Oh, will ye no come back again?"

"Haud your heed," snapped Gordon. "You've never seen the bonnie banks o' Loch Lomond in yer life. We trust you, Miss Kip, brave hound, and we'll do everything you say."

"Miaow," concurred Angus. "Never say die!"

"Look!" called one of the men working on the respraying. "A greyhound! Valuable animal that."

"Where?" asked Al Capone, who had been pacing impatiently about the yard.

"There, just running out!"

"After it, quick!" yelled Capone. "Could make a bob or two on the race tracks with that one." And he began to give chase.

Fortunately for Miss Kip and unfortunately for Al Capone he collided with the paint man, complete with sprayer, and got covered in strong-smelling pink paint.

44

"Can't anyone ever look where they're going?" shouted Al Capone, furious.

"Job's done now, guv," said the other man.

"Best be on our way, " called Sid from the driver's seat.

"No trouble," said Bert.

"Oh, very well," said Capone, and got back into the vehicle. "Suppose we'd better off-load this lot. Slimey'll be expecting us."

"No trouble," said Bert.

Miss Kip was waiting for them round the corner. As soon as she thought she wouldn't be spotted she ran out and started tracking the lorry again. She had been glad of the break in the yard as it had been a good ten miles from Primrose Hill. She hoped it wouldn't be much further now.

As she ran a stream of puzzling questions went through her mind. Why had the cats been captured in the first place; what was going to happen to them? Nothing pleasant, of that she was sure. Where were they going, how far and what would she do when they reached their destination? How could she rescue all those cats, single-pawed so to speak? So far she had formed no definite plan. For the time all she could do was concentrate on keeping up with the lorry and hope, when they stopped, some opportunity would present itself.

She was getting tired now; her heart pounded in her chest and her breath came in quick pants. When she realised the lorry was about to join a motorway and saw the signs '70 m.p.h. No learner drivers' she was really worried. Even Miss Kip, the Fastest Paw in the West, couldn't go that fast.

Fortunately Sid did not like driving over 40 m.p.h. whether on a motorway or not. In fact, luckily for Miss Kip, he drove even more slowly on motorways than on ordinary roads.

"Got nicely out of that one then," said Al Calpone, but he didn't sound as confident as usual. "New number plates, new colour. They'll never catch us now. Pity we didn't get more of them nasty furry moggies but that's business."

"No trouble," said Bert.

"Your boss, Smiley, ain't going to like it though, is he?" said Sid. "All them cats, there for the collecting and you come back with a measly handful. What'll you tell him?"

"Say we was misinformed," answered Al Capone. "Our source exaggerated, that's what."

"No trouble," confirmed Bert, and nodded his head fiercely. No one noticed his woolly cap had lost its bobble.

"Can't you ever say anything else, you great fool?" said Al Capone irritably. "No trouble, nonsense! There'll be plenty of trouble if Slimey gets to know what really happened. He'll think one of us grassed or something. How did the Fuzz get there anyway, I'd like to know?"

"Couldn't be Fred or Harry, I'd vouch for them any day," said Sid. "Must have been just bad luck. Cops come to investigate something else and saw us."

"No trouble," muttered Bert.

"It's a silly name to call a company, Catskins Ltd," mused Al Capone, pushing his trilby to the back of his head. "After all, the business is illegal and you'd think Slimey'd want to disguise the operation. Call it Fantasy Furs or Softwear Products or something like that."

"Well, he can be pretty stupid sometimes for all his big talk," said Sid. "Can't add up, I know that. Can come in pretty useful, mind, if you're working for him like. But he's a good business-man for all that. Makes a packet out of his furs, I'm told, and sells the skinned carcasses off as rabbit meat."

"And if that fails, off go the bones to the glue factory," added Al Capone. "Yes, he's got an eye for a good business, true enough."

The cats, ears pricked, listened in horror to the fate that was planned for them.

"Horrible," said Gordon, his grey fur rising on his back.

"Oh, that I had never left ma wee home in the West," wailed Wee Willie White Paws.

"Will ye stop yer moaning, Willie! We'll fight 'em tooth and claw," growled Angus, yellow eyes blazing.

"Miss Kip will think of a way out, I'm sure," said Flora, who was small and fawn-coloured.

"Listen," said Gordon, "they're talking again."

Al Capone and Sid were having a conversation, it was true,

about money and how they weren't paid enough. Bert made his usual contribution.

"No trouble," he said.

"If you say that again I'll crown you," shouted Al Capone, making Bert start sideways and bump into Sid who nearly swerved off onto the hard shoulder.

"Watch what you're doing," Sid yelled. "We were nearly a gonner then. Remember we're on a motorway."

"Enough, I've had enough!" shouted Al Capone. "Can't stand another minute. Look, Services in one mile. Pull in, Sid, and we'll have a cup of coffee."

"But what about getting to Slimey's in time to get all them cats skinned and ready for fur coats by morning?" said Sid. "He'll kill us if we're late."

"And I'll kill *you* if you don't turn in now! There's the last sign; quick or we'll be too late and there won't be another one for miles."

"No trouble," said Bert.

"Oh, very well," said Sid. "Don't know why I worry anyway. I've done my bit driving. Rest is nothing to do with me, thank goodness."

And putting on his indicator he took the left fork that led to the motorway services area.

Miss Kip, greatly relieved that they were going to stop again, followed at a discreet distance. As soon as she saw the three men go inside the building where the café was she ran over to the van.

"Gordon, Angus, Wee Willie, Flora," she barked, "I'm here, outside the van. Stand by to escape."

"Oh noble hound," said Gordon. "We're ready."

An iron bar secured the back of the lorry. Miss Kip hoped she'd have the strength to move it. She jumped up and with her long, black nose pushed at the bar with all her might and main. At last it shot up and fell back with a heavy clank. She prayed no one would hear it and come to investigate. Luckily all the travellers were too intent on their own business to bother.

Inside, the cats rallied together to push the doors open. Finally they gave and the animals all fell out in a heap.

"Come on," said Kip, "no time to waste. They'll be back soon. That bar took some moving."

"Oh, and you've hurt your nose," said Flora. "Shall I lick it better for you?"

"Not now," replied Miss Kip. "Anyway, I've got to get this bar back in position. Don't want them to smell a rat, if you'll pardon the expression."

"Quite," said Gordon.

"Now," barked Miss Kip, "you see that big bridge inside the building. What we've got to do, without attracting too much notice, is run over that to the other side of the motorway and then hitch a lift back to London."

"We'll never make it; we're doomed. We'll be gloves by morning," moaned Wee Willie.

"Oh, fleas to you," growled Angus sharply. "Where's your

spirit, cat? You deserve to be gloves with all your miaowing and wailing."

"Right, we're ready, Miss Kip. Best paws forward, cats," said Gordon.

"You and Flora lead the way," Kip instructed him, "and I'll go at the back in case there's trouble. I can always hold off human interference for a bit by raising my hackles, growling and baring my teeth."

"But you've got such a kind face, Miss Kip," said Flora, "surely no one would take you seriously?"

"Want to bet," said Kip, and in a trice she had turned into a monstrous hound with flashing eyes and slavering jaws, her lips curled back and her great canine teeth flashing like ivory daggers.

The cats crouched down and drew back on their haunches in alarm.

"Fantastic, Kip," said Gordon. "Enough to frighten anyone. Come on, cats! Forward!"

Led by Gordon and Flora, the Gallant 99 ran across the car park and into the big building with its shops and toilets and telephones. Luckily the café was a bit further back so there was no danger of them being spotted by Al Capone, Bert or Sid. Up the stairs they scampered and across the long bridge.

"Look at those cars, how fast they're going," squeaked a kitten, stopping and pressing his nose to the glass that enclosed the bridge. "Were we going like that?"

"Not quite," said Angus, giving him a cuff with his paw. "No time for dawdling. Off you go."

There were a few human beings crossing the bridge and lots of them in the hallways but no one took much notice of the cats. They all seemed pre-occupied. No one tried to stop them and Miss Kip had no need to put on her Hound of the Baskervilles act, as she called it. The Hound of the Baskervilles was, as you may remember, an extremely fierce animal who terrorised Dartmoor in Devon and whose secret was discovered by that famous detective Sherlock Holmes with his friend Doctor Watson.

Down the stairs on the opposite side the cats ran, past the

shop where that morning's newspapers were just being delivered, hot from the press, and out into the car park.

It was March the 21st, the first day of Spring, and dawn was breaking in the eastern sky.

"The cats will be setting off any minute," said Gordon. "Madoc told us to have our faces washed and our fur licked for a daybreak start."

"Oh, what'll we do," wailed Wee Willie. "We're too late. Even though we have escaped we can't join the march. Oh, woe is us. Miaow, miaow, oh woe!"

"Haud yer heed, yer miserable bundle of moaning fur and whimpering whiskers," snapped Angus. "We can catch them up. Hitch a lift to Downing Street itself. Mebbe an MP'll give us a ride. They must always be driving up from their constituencies to go gassing in that great House people are always talking about."

"Good thinking, Angus," said Gordon. "We'll make it somehow, even if we have to split up. We can't let Hamish down."

"He'll be worried out of his fur and whiskers," said Flora. "Do you think they realise we were trapped to make fur coats?"

"He's pretty sharp is Hamish McPurr," said Gordon, "and, of course, it's happened before. Remember that case of the Glasgow Growlers not all that long ago? Entire clan of cats rounded up in the Gorbals in one night. Never seen again."

"Oh, wretched animals," wailed Wee Willie.

Miss Kip was getting agitated.

"This is where I leave you," she told the cats. "I've got to get back across that bridge and catch the lorry before it leaves."

"But why, Miss Kip?" asked Flora, worried.

"I've got to trail them to their headquarters," said the grey-hound softly. "That's the only way we'll bring them to justice."

Angus growled.

"But they might kill you," protested Flora.

"That't a risk I've got to take," said the brave hound. "Catskins Ltd, you say they call themselves?"

"That's what I thought I heard," said Gordon. "Quite a big organisation from the sound of it."

50

Angus growled again. "I hope they all get fleas, great big ones with large appetites."

"Well, we'll have left a few in that van anyway," said Flora. "Let's hope they make a meal of the three of them."

"Goodbye then, Miss Kip, and the best o' luck tae ye," said Gordon. "We'll have paws and whiskers crossed for your safety. Don't take any risks."

"Goodbye, cats," barked Kip, and sped off like a streak of golden lightning towards the bridge.

"Brave animal," said Gordon. "And now to our lift. Flora, you and Wee Willie take that side of the car park and me and Angus'll take this. If you get a life miaow as loud as you can and we'll do the same."

It was the most difficult thing the cats had had to do. No one seemed to want ninety-nine cats in the back of the car.

"I love cats," one woman told Flora and Wee Willie, "and if you all had baskets to travel in, or even a big blanket to lie on, well, that would be a different matter altogether. But I can't possibly have your sharp claws on my nice upholstery. It'd bring down the value of the car overnight."

Others were rude; some aggressive. One man threw stones at them and caught Angus a nasty blow blow on the shoulder.

"Filthy, furry, flea-ridded creatures," he yelled. "Out of my way."

The Gallant 99 were beginning to despair.

"Perhaps we should try and walk it," said Angus, licking his injured shoulder.

"It'd take days," said Gordon. "We'd never get there till the whole thing was over."

"What did I tell ye?" growled Wee Willie. "We're doomed, doomed."

"Oh, stop being such a misery," miaowed Flora, and gave him a sharp cuff across the whiskers. "We'll think of something. We'll try again. Look, there's a nice big van drawing up near the café. Let's try that."

"The driver looks a good sort," said Gordon as he and Flora approached on soft paws.

"And he's got three children with him," purred Flora. "That

could be a good sign."

"Excuse me, sir," said Gordon in his very best voice. "Any chance of a lift to London? Only we were cat-napped and we've got to get to a march."

"It's the march of the Steel Town Cats on Downing Street," explained Flora, as both the man and the children seemed to be looking sympathetic. "We're taking a petition to the Prime Minister to ask her to give us work."

"We've been made redundant, see," added Gordon. "From the Steel Works." He couldn't quite understand why the man and the three children were looking so surprised. And whereas everybody else they had approached had responded quickly – albeit not very helpfully – to their request, this lot seemed dumb-founded.

"Perhaps they're deaf and dumb," whispered Flora. "Try sign language with your paws."

Gordon started a series of extraordinary gesticulations. The children burst out laughing.

"They're Steel Town Cats," said Tessa.

"They must be colleagues of our lot," said David.

"Didn't you have a map?" asked Richard. "I made one for our cats."

"Oh, they're not deaf and dumb after all," said Flora, rather embarrassed at having forced Gordon to make such an exhibition of himself.

"You're part of Madoc the Magnificent's Mousers' March, are you?" asked Sam, finding the full title rather a mouthful. He had driven a long way that morning and had been looking forward to his coffee break at the motorway café before driving into central London with the children to see the march.

"That's right," said Gordon, "only we were cat-napped."

"For fur coats," growled Angus, who had joined them.

"And if it hadn't been for Miss Kip," said Flora, "the golden greyhound . . ."

"Fastest Paw in the West," interrupted Gordon.

"We'd never have got away," concluded Flora.

"Miss Kip?" asked Sam, worried. "What did she do; where is she now?"

52

Briefly Gordon told him what had happened and how brave Miss Kip had decided to follow the gang and bring them to justice.

"So that every cat can walk free with his tail held high," said Angus.

"I do hope she'll be all right," said Sam. "I love that dog so much. She's been with us since she was only five weeks old."

"Her mother died," explained David.

"And we had to feed her every two hours," added Tessa.

"She's a sensible animal," said Gordon. "I'm sure she won't take any unnecessary risks."

"I suppose not," said Sam, but he was worried about his dog. "However, the thing to do now is to get you lot to London. The Gallant 99, are you? Well, hop in."

It didn't take long for Sam to get to London – he drove rather faster than Sid – and he dropped the cats in Trafalgar Square.

"It's not far from here," he told Gordon. "Up Whitehall and turn right, you can't miss it. I'll find somewhere to park and we'll see you later."

"Purr," said Gordon, "and thanks a million."

"Oh, look at those great big stone cats," squeaked a kitten. "Are there really cats as big as that?"

"Yes," purred Flora, "they're called lions, the big cats; all part of our noble family, of course."

"Oh, look, Flora, he's waving to us with his paw," miaowed the kitten in excitement.

"So he is," said Flora, "wishing us luck, I expect."

"All fall into line!" commanded Gordon o' the Glens. "Remember we're the Gallant 99. Now which way is Whitehall?"

"It must be a place with big buildings," suggested Angus.

"Yes, I suppose it must," agreed Gordon. "But there are big buildings everywhere. I've never seen anything like it."

"Excuse me, sir, if I can be of help . . ." The voice was so small, especially against the roar of the traffic, that Gordon couldn't see at first where it came from.

"It's me, Wee Jock Ginger Socks," said the voice. "I'm from Scotland, too, but I live here now with an actress. I can lead you to Downing Street if you'll allow."

Jock was well named for, although an adult cat, he was tiny. Also, most unusually, he was white all over with four ginger paws. Generally it's the other way round, as you know.

"That's most civil of you, Jock," said Gordon. "And it makes us a hundred animals again – our leader Hamish McPurr is not with us at the moment – so that means we can sing our marching song 'Wi' a hundred mousers'. Lead on, Wee Jock Ginger Socks!"

The tiny cat led them across the square to a wide road, at the end of which the cats could see Big Ben and the Houses of Parliament. The London traffic stopped to make way for them and as they marched they sang their song.

> "Wi' a hundred mousers and aw and aw,
> Come one, we'll gi' them a claw, a claw,
> Never say you're beat or drop paw, drop paw,
> Until ye lay down and dee."

Outside Number 10 Downing Street Hamish McPurr pricked up his ears.

"Our marching song, 'Wi' a hundred mousers'! They've escaped!"

Before long the one hundred marching mousers (the Gallant 99 plus one) had rounded the corner and when they saw them, best paws forward and tails erect, an ear-piercing caterwaul went up from all the waiting animals.

Soon Gordon o' the Glens was telling Hamish and Madoc all that had happened since they were cat-napped the night before. How Al Capone and his gang had planned to take them to Slimey Jim to be made into fur coats, how Miss Kip had rescued them and how Sam and the children had found them stranded at the motorway service station. It all seemed years ago now they were safely united with their colleagues.

"What a brave animal that Miss Kip is," purred Madoc. "I do hope she'll be all right."

Patchwork, who had been missing during the latter part of this conversation, was pushing his way through the crowd towards Madoc. His rug-like coat looked more dishevelled than ever.

"News from Miss Kip," he announced in breathless miaows. "She's sent out an SOS for help. Constable Tuck picked it up on his walkie-talkie and he and Titch are going to the scene of the crime."

"What crime?" asked Madoc.

"Well, I'm not sure yet," said Patchwork, "but I liked the phrase. Anyway, skinning cats must be a crime, surely?"

"Thank goodness she's getting help," said Madoc. "We must all cross our paws and our whiskers for her and pray to the Great Cat in the Sky for her safety."

"Purr," agreed the cats, and settled down on their haunches to concentrate.

CHAPTER TEN

THE cats had been sitting outside Number 10 Downing Street for about half an hour when the door opened and Augustus, the pin-striped cat, appeared on the step.

"Madoc, my good cat," he called across the road in his superior miaow. "My mistress can give you half an hour now before she goes to the House. Come on, chop-chop, no dawdling!"

At the first miaow Madoc had leapt to his paws and he was across the road before you could say 'Kippers'. He was not an animal to let the grass grow under his paws, but Augustus was determined to keep the advantage.

"Come on, come on," he said, feigning impatience. "You're a most fortunate animal. *People* sometimes have to wait days for an audience but I, with my special influence, have managed to secure you an immediate appointment. I hope I shall be rewarded in the usual manner . . ." And he gave Madoc a most meaningful look.

"Yes, yes, of course," said Madoc, but he didn't know at all what Augustus meant. An old herring bone from a dustbin would hardly accord with Augustus's idea of a suitable reward.

Augustus showed Madoc into a room on the first floor. It was a big room with a long table surrounded by at least twenty chairs. On a carver in the middle sat an elegant lady of middle years. Before her was a mound of papers and an open dispatch box. She was writing busily.

"I thought I gave instructions not to be disturbed," she said, looking up crossly. But her expression changed when she saw the cats. "Oh, it's you, Augustus dear, you good and handsome cat. Yes, bring your furry visitor over here."

"Good morning, Prime Minister," said Madoc politely.

"Have you had a chance to consider our petition?"

"Well, yes, I have, Mr Cat – or may I call you Madoc?"

"Yes, purr."

"I have given it deep thought and will, indeed, continue to do so, but I simply cannot think of any work to offer you at the present moment in time. As Augustus has probably told you, modern poisons have, to a large extent, replaced cats as vermin exterminators and in the future cats will have to learn to look on themselves more as leisure objects than workers. It's much the same with humans."

"But Mrs Prime Minister," Madoc interrupted, "the mice and rats get used to poison and it doesn't work any more. I assure you, the country is crawling with vermin and we will be only too pleased to dispose of them for you in return for the occasional tin of catfood, tasty scraps and a passing saucer of milk. As I'm sure I have no need to point out to you – you being a cat owner and all . . " Here he looked at Augustus who had jumped onto an empty plinth, the better to look down his nose, and was eyeing Madoc with scornful green eyes. "As I am sure you know, Madoc continued, "cats cannot live by mice alone. They are pretty disgusting as food, actually, and with the poisons and other rubbish they eat nowadays they are not much good for our health either. Nor, I might add, for yours, Mrs Prime Minister."

"I'm sure you have a point there, Madoc," said the Prime Minister with a shudder. "But I really cannot believe there is much vermin about these days, certainly not in *this* area at any rate. Why, I don't think Augustus has *ever* caught a mouse in his life."

Augustus's shiver of disgust at the thought nearly sent him toppling off his pedestal but he managed, with difficulty, to regain his balance.

Madoc was not in the least surprised Augustus had never caught a mouse and he nearly said as much but he managed to restrain himself in time.

"Well, Mrs Prime Minister," he said instead, "if we can prove to you that there *are* mice and rats, even in Number 10, will you believe us then?"

"I suppose so," answered the PM reluctantly, "but I think you're wasting your time."

"What time will you be back from the House tonight?" asked Madoc, a plan forming in his mind.

"About midnight, I expect," answered the PM, "unless, of course, we have an all-night sitting. But I think we'll be all right tonight. I hope so; I'm dreadfully tired, though I wouldn't dream of admitting it to anyone but you two."

"No, of course not," said Madoc with understanding. He knew what it was to be a leader. "Well, I'll be here at midnight and by breakfast time tomorrow morning I guarantee I'll have a catch for you."

'I hope not,' thought the Prime Minister, but she said "Very well. But even if you catch five hundred mice I can still not guarantee work, you know. Catfood and milk are very expensive these days and they were not accounted for in the recent budget. We can't take on expenditure not budgeted for, you do realise that."

"Midnight," said Madoc, stretching out a white paw.

"Midnight," confirmed the Prime Minister.

CHAPTER ELEVEN

WHEN Madoc emerged from Number 10 Hamish and Patchwork told him how Sam had organised accommodation for them underneath the arches on the embankment.

"He's arranged to meet us there with supplies," said Patchwork. "It's traditionally where all the tramps sleep but Sam says he's had a word with them and they're quite happy to share their space with us. Reckon we'll keep them warm."

"And a couple of policemen have been put on duty on the bridge so we won't be attacked again by those villains from Catskins Ltd," added Hamish.

"Good," said Madoc. "*Da iawn.* Excellent. But what about Miss Kip, the golden greyhound, and our friends Titch and Tuck? Any news of them?"

"Yes," said Hamish, "the Downing Street duty policeman said he'd heard on the walkie-talkie they were on to a big racket."

"Couldn't be Catskins Ltd, could it?" asked Madoc.

"Well naturally I asked," replied Hamish, "but he wouldn't say. Just said they reported they were on to a big crime-busting operation and would be in touch later."

"Let's hope Miss Kip's tracked them down and that she's come to no harm," said Madoc with a growl. "They're very tenacious, greyhounds, but there's a limit to the running any animal can do, even the Fastest Paw in the West. And I keep worrying they may have guns."

"She'll be all right, I'm sure," Patchwork reassured him. But he was worried too now. He hadn't thought about guns. "Perhaps Sam can ring the police for us and find out something?" he suggested.

"Good thinking, Patchwork," said Madoc. "Now, let's get

down to those quarters on the embankment, get some food inside ourselves and make our plans. I could do with a bite or two. It was pretty hard, I can tell you, having to sniff that spoilt Augustus's liver luncheon and not be able to get paws on it myself."

They followed Patchwork across a bridge, down some steps and along a wide pathway that led to a park. Tall modern buildings towered behind them and across the water they could see, in one direction, the spires of the Houses of Parliament and Big Ben and, in the other, the stately dome of St Paul's Cathedral.

Sam and the children were waiting for them with hundreds of tins of catfood and several bottles of milk. Cat lovers from all over the capital had rallied to the animals' cause and donations poured in as fast as Sam, Tessa, David and Richard could open and serve them. There were also some special scraps from Owain Butcher that Sam had brought up in a cool container.

After the feast there was complete silence for about half an hour as every cat washed fur and whiskers clean. Then Madoc put forward his plan.

"Tonight I want each one of you, cat and kitten, to catch at least one rat or mouse. Then, by 8 a.m. prompt, you must all be lined up outside Number 10 with your spoils. The only rule is that your prey must be caught within a two-mile radius of Number 10. Any questions?"

"What about the local cats?" asked one ginger tom. "Won't they object to us moving in on their territory?"

"I doubt it," said Madoc wryly. "They're a lazy lot round here. Fed on the fat of the land most of them and can't tell the difference between a mouse and a mole."

"Well, they do taste pretty much the same," mused Patchwork, but he was quelled with a withering glance from his chief.

"Right? Right," said Madoc. "I myself will take up my post within Number 10 and endeavour to catch a fine specimen. Good mousing to you all!"

"Good mousing!" The miaow went up from the crowd and spontaneously they burst into their campaigning song.

"Steel Town Cats we'll fight like tigers,
Sabre-toothed and claws well sharpened,
Spit and scratch and snarl and bite
And we shall win the day!"

The spring sunshine had grown stronger by now and the cats stretched out along the riverside, taking advantage of the warmth.

Madoc, Patchwork and Hamish took the opportunity to go for a stroll and discuss their plan of action.

"She was quite sympathetic really," Madoc told his two friends. "Cat lover, of course, but she didn't hold out any real hope of work. Even if we prove London is overrun by mice – which my whiskers assure me it is – I don't suppose that'll persuade her to give us employment. She keeps wittering on about the budget. Catching a rat or mouse each and presenting them to her first thing tomorrow morning will help but we need to come up with something else, something that isn't affected by the budget estimates, something that'll capture the sympathy of the people and get her returned at the next election. Something useful but imaginative, something . . ." And his voice trailed off into a thoughtful purr.

Patchwork and Hamish recognised the mood and crouching, like Madoc, on their haunches they purred the slow, quiet purr of concentration. Their eyes gazed lazily across the water as they thought and thought.

Their reverie was broken by a high-pitched squawk from a tree above.

"Good Lord, Peter Puffin, or may my feathers be oiled," shrilled Petula Pigeon. "Whatever are you doing here so far from home?"

"You may well ask," answered Peter Puffin with a sigh, turning to preen his glossy black and white feathers. "We've been evicted. Happens all the time these days. Hardly an island left to nest on. Wherever you go round the coast it's always the same story – rats."

"Rats?" queried Petula Pigeon with a shudder. "What about them?"

"Why," said Peter, "they're overrunning all our little

offshore islands. Couple of them stow away on a pleasure yacht or fishing boat, land on an island of puffins and before you can say 'Scratch my poll' there's a colony of them. They attack us and our chicks and eat our eggs so that if this goes on much longer we'll be extinct."

"Like the Dodo," said Petula mournfully.

"Exactly," confirmed Peter. "Like the Dodo." And both birds bent their necks in mourning for the lost bird of far-off Mauritius in the Indian Ocean.

"So what are you going to do?" asked Petula.

"I don't know, I really don't," said Peter with a deep sigh. "My own colony is roosting temporarily on one of your islands in the Thames but it's not really suitable. No decent fishing and by the time the nesting season gets under way the trippers will be out in their thousands which'll be no use to us."

"No, I can see that," said Petula. "Of course *we* quite like them. Nuts in Trafalgar Square and all that. But I appreciate it's not the same for you wild sea types."

"Well, must be getting back upstream," said Peter, ruffling his feathers. "If you think of anything let me know by pigeon post. So long. Must fly." And with a flutter of his wings he was off.

"Did you hear that?" said Madoc.

"Yes," said Patchwork with a growl. "Poor puffins. Nice, smart sort of bird, though they have got rather silly faces. Would be dreadful if they became extinct all the same."

"Like our big cousins the tigers," added Hamish. "Hardly any of them left now. Was nice to hear them growling in the zoo this morning and singing our song. Lots, of course, were killed in that terrible war in Cambodia."

"And thousands were shot in India and made into rugs," mourned Patchwork. He was very sensitive on the subject of rugs since he resembled one so nearly himself.

"Yes, but do you realise what this could mean to *us*?" persisted Madoc, tossing back his handsome black head with an impatient 'brrrp'.

"To us, with no tigers, you mean?" asked Patchwork. "Surely they wouldn't put us in zoos instead?"

"Patchwork, Patchwork, I think the march has addled your brain. It's nothing to do with tigers, *dim o gwbl*, nothing at all. Rats, Patchwork, *llygod fawr*, rats." For the last few days Madoc had been speaking English since that was the language of the majority of the marchers and, of course, of the Prime Minister. But now to make himself quite clear to Patchwork he turned back to his native tongue, Welsh. "*Llygod fawr*."

"*Llygod fawr*?" repeated Patchwork, and scratched his head.

"You mean," said Hamish, light dawning in his amber eyes, "you mean rats; we could help to get rid of them?"

"Yes, yes," said Madoc. "We would offer our services to rid Britain's offshore islands of rats. It's the Year of the Bird and you know how keen humans have become lately on conservation of species and so on. Guilty consciences about dodos and tigers, I suppose. So this would be just the sort of thing to win an election."

"Kill a Rat and Save a Puffin!" said Patchwork who always liked a good slogan.

"Exactly," said Madoc. "And the beauty of this scheme would be that poison, in this case, would be no good. Poison would kill the puffins as well as the rats so we're the only answer."

"Brilliant," said Hamish. "There are masses of islands, as you know, round the Scottish coast so there'd be plenty of work for all of us. But would they trust us with the birds? Puffin can be very tasty if you're in the mood . . ."

"We'd have to come to some agreement about that," conceded Madoc, thinking quickly now. "Sign a non-aggression pact or some such thing."

"And what about food supplies?" asked Patchwork. "Obviously we can't be expected to eat rats, not all the time at any rate. Cats cannot live by mice – or rats – alone." He intoned part of the Cats' Gospel known to all animals.

"No, indeed," said Madoc, "there'd have to be some form of ferry system that would bring us food, say, once a week."

"Or it could be airlifted," suggested Hamish.

"Yes, said Madoc, "but that could be expensive."

"At least keeping us in supplies would provide some extra jobs for humans," said Patchwork.

"And revive the fishing industry maybe," added Hamish.

"Good thinking, Hamish," said Madoc. "Let's stroll back now and have a saucer of milk and bit of a catnap and I'll put our suggestions to the Prime Minister in the morning – along with my offering!"

CHAPTER TWELVE

A T midnight Madoc returned to Number 10 Downing Street as promised. He came in through the cat flap at the back that Augustus had shown him and took up his mousing position by a cupboard under the stairs just outside the kitchen.

"Oh, it's you," said Augustus, who had come trotting downstairs when he heard the flap go. "Thought it might be my friend Peregrine from the Palace. Comes over, don't you know, to give me the latest gossip on the royal corgis. Odd sort of animal, really. Looks more like a horse than a cat. Smaller, of course. But one likes to keep in touch with the Court Circular, doesn't one?"

"I'm not sure I'm all that interested," said Madoc. And then, remembering he was a guest on another animal's mousing patch, added quickly, "But, yes, it must be fascinating. What is the Court Circular anyway?"

"It's a sort of list of royal engagements," explained Augustus, the high-bred drawl returning to his miaow. "One must know, don't you see, whether the royal corgis are holidaying in Balmoral this year and if they are to attend the Highland Games. No well-bred animal is ignorant of such matters."

"No, I suppose not," said Madoc, remembering still to follow the Mousing Courtesy Code. "Well, I'd better start work. No mouse, no parley with the Prime Minister – I trust that's the correct expression? So I'll not waste any more time."

"Oh, very well," said Augustus. "I'm off to my basket. PM's already retired but she'll be down early for breakfast. Good mousing – but I'm afraid you haven't a hope. If there *were* mice around don't you think *I'd* have caught one before now?"

"Well, yes, I suppose you would," said Madoc, but he had to

cross his paws as he knew he was telling a lie.

At about three in the morning his prey appeared. It was a great, big brown rat with long whiskers and a tail like a length of rope. As Madoc had guessed, it came from the cupboard under the stairs, squeezing itself under the gap in the bottom of the door. In the passageway it paused to sniff the air. For some minutes it sat there with its nose twitching. There was something different in the air tonight.

"A cat smell?" thought Roger to himself. Well, there was nothing strange about that. Augustus and his social-climbing friend Peregrine were nothing to worry about. But had a third cat joined them?

His whiskers twitched again, scenting danger, and he turned to go back into the cupboard. But he changed his mind.

"Don't be ridiculous," he told himself crossly. "Any friend of Augustus's *must* be useless. It's just some other lay-about Whitehall cat. Come on, Roger, you're losing your grip."

Soon poor Roger was to lose far more than that. As he stepped into the kitchen, preparing, as usual, to help himself to the exciting and varied cheese board, the cover of which was easily removed with a powerful claw and a butt of the nose, Madoc pounced.

The kill was clean and quick. From long experience Madoc knew exactly where to strike and with a snap of his jaws he broke Roger's neck. Safe now in the knowledge that no other rat or mouse would dare put paw over the threshold of Number 10 that night Madoc curled up on a mat by the Aga cooker and fell into a deep, well-earned sleep.

He was awoken by high-pitched screams and hysterical miaows. As he rubbed the sleep from his eyes an extraordinary scene came into view. Both the Prime Minister and Augustus were standing on chairs. The Prime Minister was clutching the skirts of her nightdress and satin dressing gown and was screaming "Help! Help!"

Augustus presented an even stranger sight. He was balanced on one back paw and one front paw, with his other two paws tucked up under him, looking for all the world like a two-legged cat. The fur on his neck stood up, his tail was bushy and he was

66

miaowing at the top of his lungs, hardly pausing to draw breath.

As Madoc picked up his rat and advanced with it towards them the cries of both mistress and cat grew louder.

"What on earth's going on?" It was the Prime Minister's husband, awakened from a deep sleep by the cacophony.

"Take it away, get rid of it! Oh, how horrible!"

"Miaow, miaow, miaow!"

"Don't bring it any nearer or I'll scream. For goodness sake, don't stand around gawping. Get that thing out of the house!"

"Miaow, miaow, miaow!"

"Oh, it's Madoc's rat," said the Prime Minister's husband. "Well, you *did* ask him to catch one. Clever cat! My goodness, it's a whopper too. Almost as big as you, Madoc, and bigger, I'd say, than Augustus." And taking Roger's corpse by the tail the Prime Minister's husband walked over to Augustus to compare sizes.

The miaows caught in Augustus's throat and he began to choke.

"For God's sake, take it away. Can't you see he's terrified?" screamed the Prime Mimister.

"A cat terrified of a rat? Oh, come off it," said the Prime Minister's husband. "And you're not looking too happy yourself," he added, observing his wife who had gone a pale shade of green. "Hope the Russians haven't got this kitchen bugged or you'll be the laughing stock of the world."

Many times this particular prime minister had been quoted in the Press saying she was afraid of nothing.

"Never mind about the Russians," she said now with an uncharacteristic lack of concern for a traditional enemy. "Just get *rid* of it!"

"Oh, all right, all right. I'll put it outside the front door with the rest of the rubbish," agreed her husband. "Clever cat," he said to Madoc as they walked along the passage together towards the front hall. "That useless Augustus has never caught so much as a baby shrew in his life and I've been saying for weeks we'd got rat trouble. Come on, let's get it outside."

"Right," said Madoc. "Would you like me to take it while you open the door?"

"Oh, thank you, most thoughtful," said the Prime Minister's husband. "No chance of you changing places with that silly Augustus I suppose?"

His proposition was cut short by the sight that met his eyes outside the house. All down the street were cats, each carrying in its mouth a rat or mouse.

"Good heavens," exclaimed the Prime Minister's husband. "Just look at that! I thought at first they'd all grown moustaches in the night." He took off his spectacles and wiped the lenses with his red-spotted pocket handkerchief. Then, turning back into the house, he called, "Come on, darling! Come and look at this! You'll never believe it!"

The Prime Minister and Augustus both ran to the door at his call. They took one look and then both fainted.

It was not till a couple of hours and several strong, black coffees later that the Prime Minister felt able to see Madoc.

"And you say that all these, er, rats and mice were caught within a two-mile radius of Downing Street?" she asked.

"Yes, madam, every one," purred Madoc proudly.

"Well, that certainly gives rise to great national concern," observed the Prime Minister, her composure restored now that the refuse collectors had removed all the corpses. "I shall appoint a parliamentary committee today to look into the matter. They may sit for a couple of years but you have convinced me, brave Madoc, that we do indeed have a problem on our hands."

"A couple of years, Mrs Prime Minister?" miaowed Madoc. "But we need jobs now. If we have to wait a couple of years we'll all be dead."

"Oh, surely not? What about all those mice and rats you catch?"

"Cats cannot live by mice alone," intoned Madoc. "In view of our sterling work last night I had hoped for an immediate vermin-slaying contract in the metropolis. However, if that's not possible, how about this new scheme of mine? I feel sure it would appeal to the electorate."

"We do not court popularity," the Prime Minister rebuked him sternly.

"No, of course not," said Madoc, "but it can help. Look, here's my plan."

And in swift purrs and urgent miaows Madoc outlined the plan he had formed with Patchwork and Hamish to free Britain's offshore islands of vermin and restore them to the puffin, the curlew and the cormorant.

"Yes, I see," said the Prime Minister, counting votes. "And it is, of course, the Year of the Bird. What a brilliant idea! However did I think of it?"

"We would, of course," continued Madoc, wondering how his idea had suddenly become someone else's, "be prepared to put our paws to a non-aggression treaty with the birds. Any cat caught violating the treaty would be banished instantly to the mainland."

"Good Heavens," said the Prime Minister, looking at her watch, "how the time has flown! I have to be in the House in an hour's time. I promise I will put this suggestion to my colleagues this very afternoon and if they are in agreement, as I feel sure they all will be, emergency legislation will be put through to enable you and your friends to start on this admirable project straight away."

"Oh, purr," said Madoc.

"And I don't see why we couldn't arrange for some of your number to stay behind and de-mouse the metropolis," continued the Prime Minister, who was beginning to think she had been rather harsh – and foolish – with Madoc earlier. "After all, a matter like that doesn't really need to be sat on by a committee for two years, does it? And I'm sure we can draw on the Contingency Fund to supply your wages and thus not interfere with the budget at all."

"Isn't that what you use for wars and things like that?" asked Madoc innocently.

"Well, yes, I suppose it is," replied the Prime Minister. "But this *is* a war," she continued, now totally convinced of the need for a Metropolitan Force of Mousers, "a War on Vermin."

"Yes, quite," agreed Madoc.

"And Madoc," added the Prime Minister, a softness coming into her voice, "I'd be grateful if you'd say nothing about that incident with your rat and the chair and me fainting. I hate to think what the Press would make of it."

"Yes, purr, I quite understand. My lips are forever sealed. You have the word of Madoc the Magnificent on that."

"Thank you; you're a good cat."

The Prime Minister showed Madoc to the door and began to prepare herself for a busy afternoon.

CHAPTER THIRTEEN

"Y OU bunch of half-wits, you good-for-nothing oafs, you . . ." For once Slimey Jim was lost for words.

"Out of five thousand cats you mean to tell me you didn't get one decent cat skin?"

"'fraid so," said Al Capone, his wide-brimmed hat now torn at the edges and his raincoat dirtier than ever.

"Well, how in heaven's name did you manage it?"

"No trouble," said Bert, who was missing the bobble on his woolly hat. "No trouble."

"Obviously," said Slimey Jim, but the sarcasm was lost on Bert. "Well, OK," he continued, "let's go through it step by step. Out of five thousand cats you manage to net only ninety-nine. You then lose the ninety-nine, *you* say, somewhere between Primrose Hill and Catskins Ltd. And you tell me the back of the lorry was fastened? So how, in the name of Lucifer, did they get away?"

"There were a couple of policemen that chased us on Primrose Hill," supplied Al Capone, "but I don't think they could possibly have got our number. We had too good a start on them. Then, of course, we changed the number plates in Sid's yard so even if they had got our number we'd be OK."

"And no one followed you, you're sure of that?"

"No trouble," said Bert.

"Saw nothing in the driving mirror," added Sid, "and heard no warning on me CB set."

"And then," pursued Slimey, "you arrive here at Catskins Ltd and, lo and behold, there's nothing there. They've all vanished, ninety-nine cats all gone. And you tell me you fastened the back and didn't stop anywhere on the way? You came straight here?"

71

"Well, in a manner of speaking, not to put too fine a point on it, perhaps we didn't exactly go *straight*. Straight, that is, to Catskins Ltd," said Al Capone, looking shifty.

"What do you mean 'in a manner of speaking', 'not to put too fine a point on it'? Did you, in plain English, or did you not stop anywhere?"

"No trouble," said Bert.

"Oh, shut up, you," yelled Slimey Jim, knocking an ashtray and a mug of congealing coffee onto the floor. "Did you or did you not stop?"

"Well," said Al Capone, removing his hat, running his fingers through his greasy hair, and giving his head a good scratch, "it was a cold night, see, and we was bitter what with waiting for those damn cats to settle down, so we thought as how we'd take a bit of a warmer, just to see us on our way like."

"What do you mean, warmer?" demanded Slimey, his face red and sweaty with rage.

"Well, like a cup of coffee and a plate of chips," admitted Al Capone at last. "We was freezing, boss, honest we was and we couldn't see as how those moggies could come to any harm for just five minutes in the car park."

"But they obviously did," said Slimey, "and now you've shopped us all, for whoever let them out of the lorry must have got the new number of the vehicle and, knowing that, must have followed you here to Catskins Ltd. So now our whole valuable business is blown thanks to you three idiots."

"But we didn't notice anyone following us, honest we didn't," said driver Sid, scratching under his arm. "I'd have *seen* them."

"Perhaps," ventured Al Capone, "the back was not done up proper and they just fell out onto the road and then while we're in the café having our warmer some bloke just comes along and shuts it up again."

"Pigs might fly," said Slimey drily. "Now you're sure, all three of you, you weren't followed?"

"Well, I did see a sort of dog around, now you mention it," said Al Capone, scratching again. It seemed he'd caught fleas from somewhere. "But dogs can't be informers, can they?"

"What sort of dog?" demanded Slimey. "Not a bloodhound by any chance?"

"No, a sort of greyhound," answered Al Capone. "Golden looking. Saw it in Sid's yard as a matter of fact. Thought I'd try and catch it and put it in for a race or two but it give me the slip."

"No trouble," confirmed Bert, also scratching. Angus's wish for the three of them had obviously been fulfilled.

"Well, that's it then," said Slimey. "Somehow this wretched greyhound has turned grass. Goodness knows how, but then goodness knows how you managed to lose ninety-nine cats in the space of forty miles."

"No trouble," said Bert.

"I know that, you buffoon," expostulated Slimey. "But the point is we're finished. Where are those two other idiots, Harry and Fred?"

"Downstairs playing cards," supplied Al Capone. "While they waits for skins, see."

"Oh, I despair," groaned Slimey. "All we can do now is scarper. Get all the spare cat skins together, dismantle the machinery and let's get packed up and off as soon as possible."

By the time they had loaded all the incriminating evidence in Sid's lorry, which had been given yet another set of new number plates as well as another fresh coat of quick-drying paint, it was early afternoon. About the same time, in fact, that Madoc the Magnificent was having his first interview with the Prime Minister. Sid was revving the lorry's engine and Al Capone, Bert, Harry and Fred were just running out of the house with the last loads of cat skins, followed by Slimey Jim carrying the filing cabinet where he kept all the names of his clients, when they heard the police sirens.

"Stop! Police!" roared PC Tuck, jumping out of the police car.

"Oh, no, you don't," said Titch, reaching up almost as high as he could to catch Slimey Jim, who had started running in the opposite direction, by the collar. "You're under arrest. I must caution you that anything you say will be taken down and may be used in evidence."

"I'm not saying nothing," stuttered Slimey. "It's nothing to do with me. It's them lot. They caught the cats, took the skins and everything. I'm just someone who's come to look at the house. It's for sale, see."

"For sale, is it?" said Titch. "So where's the 'For Sale' notice?"

"Private, see," said Slimey, grasping at straws. "Just a private deal between me and the owner. Here are the particulars." And he bumped his chin on top of the filing cabinet that he was still clutching.

"Oh yes," said Titch, "shall we have a look then?"

"Oh, no need for that," said Slimey. "In fact I'm in a bit of a hurry, so if you don't mind I'll just be getting along."

"You'll be getting nowhere except down to the Station with us," warned Titch. "Now let's have a look at that box."

Slimey was just about to try and run off again when a cold, wet nose touched his bare arm. Letting out a yell he dropped the cabinet and then yelled again, even louder, for the heavy case had fallen right on the big toe in which he had gout.

"Oh, what was that? I'm in agony. Get me to hospital quickly," he cried. Then he saw to whom the nose belonged. It was Miss Kip, the golden greyhound. "So it *was* that blasted hound after all that shopped us. Never liked greyhounds, anyway, not since the day I lost a thousand smackers on one at the White City. Nasty, nosey, lot."

"Come along now," said Titch.

"Oh, all right," said Slimey, and allowed himself to be led away to the waiting police car.

By this time Tuck, with the help of some other officers, had got the remaining five Catskin employees in handcuffs.

"Think this bobble incriminates the one with the woolly hat straight away," he told his colleague. "Almost grabbed it from me when he saw it, muttering something like 'No trouble' all the time."

"Yes, that'll be Exhibit One," said Titch. "But that lorry is packed with stuff including, I'm afraid, several hundred cat skins. There'll be more exhibits at this trial than there are in the National Gallery."

"Well, we'd best be off," said Tuck. "Come on, Miss Kip, we'll get you back to Sam and your feline friends. They certainly have a lot to thank you for."

"Bark," answered Miss Kip. "Bark, bark." And she flopped exhausted onto the back seat of the police car.

CHAPTER FOURTEEN

MADOC and his friends could not believe their good fortune. The House of Commons gave its immediate and unanimous approval to the 'Catch a Rat and Save a Puffin' scheme and the House of Lords ratified it the same day. Never in the history of parliament had a decision been arrived at with such speed.

"I've put the Minister for the Environment in charge of the whole scheme and he will be working out details this week," the Prime Minister told Madoc when they met in her sitting room at Number 10 that evening.

"Thank you, Prime Minister, a thousand purrs," said Madoc. "My cats can't wait to get to work and get their paws on those greedy rats."

"You've asked some good mousers to stay behind and rid the city of this menace, I trust?" asked the Prime Minister. "Before you brought the matter to my attention so vividly" – and here she shuddered – "I had no *idea* there were so many mice and rats about. Quite obviously, as you so perceptively pointed out, they have become immune to poison."

"It would seem so, Prime Minister," said Madoc, giving his fur a quick lick. When a cat is paid a compliment or proved right in some matter he usually does this, as you've probably noticed.

"Yes," he continued, "five hundred of my brother and sister mousers from the Midlands have agreed to undertake Operation Mousehunt. No doubt you will reward them in the usual manner?" By this time Madoc had picked up quite a number of Augustus's choice expressions.

"Naturally," concurred the Prime Minister. "The Contingency Fund will provide."

"Quite," said Madoc.

"Perhaps you know of an animal who would move in here?" An anxious note had crept into the Prime Minister's voice. "I'm sure Augustus would have no objection, would you, Augustus?"

"No, purr, I wouldn't," said Augustus, who since the rat-catching episode had become a much humbler and pleasanter animal.

"Leave it to me," said Madoc. "I know just the animal for you. Katie Cat. She was in domestic service once. Thoroughly housetrained, you understand, and a most conscientious mouser. Also she's had an operation so she won't have any kittens which *you* would probably consider an advantage."

"Well, yes, that *is* preferable in a busy place like Number 10," said the Prime Minister. "What colour is she?"

"Black and white like Augustus," answered Madoc, "only not quite so pin-striped, if you see what I mean."

"She sounds ideal," said the Prime Minister. "What do you think, Augustus?"

"Purr," said Augustus. "Good idea. I'll be happy to welcome her to our establishment."

"Good, well that's settled. Tell Katie Cat, Madoc, that she can move in as soon as she likes."

"Thank you, Prime Minister, I'll do that. I know she'll be delighted," said Madoc.

"It seems," continued the Prime Minister, "that this whole business will not only save the puffins – and, of course, you cats – but it will also provide jobs for voters; er, I mean people."

"Oh, please, please, Mrs Prime Minister, could my friend Sam – you know, the one I told you about – could he have one of them?" begged Madoc.

"Why, yes, of course," answered the Prime Minister. "He can be Project Controller, North Wales Region. And if you have any other friends who'd be interested we'll need people to buy, collect and distribute your cat food. We'll need butchers, packers and lorry drivers, office staff and secretaries, and fishermen and trawler skippers too. Then we'll have to have scientists and naturalists monitoring the progress of the puffins . . . Oh, but before I forget," the Prime Minister interrupted herself, "here's the Non-Aggression Treaty (Birds) that you have to sign. The House insists."

"Certainly," said Madoc, and jumping onto the desk he put his right paw in the saucer of ink provided and made a neat pawmark on the parchment before him.

"Thank you," said the Prime Minister. "And that's witnessed by myself and Augustus. Now don't forget to blot your paw before you jump onto the carpet."

He was just making sure that the last trace of ink had left his paw when a loud booming noise startled him and he jumped to the floor, almost upsetting the ink saucer in the process.

"Oh, there's the gong for supper," said the Prime Minister. "You *will* join us for a little light refreshment, won't you, Madoc?"

"Yes, purr," replied Madoc, somewhat shaken by the near catastrophe with the ink saucer, "I'd be delighted."

After supper – pilchards in tomato sauce followed by braised liver and creamy rice pudding – Madoc said goodbye to the Prime Minister and Augustus and made his way back to his companions on the embankment. Their whereabouts that night was no secret to the whole city. Their joyous miaows could be heard for miles around.

In the morning Sam and the children came to collect Madoc, Patchwork, Esmeralda the Efficient and as many other cats as would fit in the van.

Rufus the Ratcatcher had accepted the job offered to him by the manager of the Motorway Services Station and had also persuaded him to take on Snowy Tom as his deputy, on the strict understanding that Snowy would do at least three hours mousing a day and smarten himself up so as not to offend customers. It was not exactly the life of ease Snowy had had in mind for himself but at least the food would be good and plentiful and there'd be somewhere nice and warm to sleep.

"I'll miss you all," said Rufus, wiping his eye with his paw, "but this is a marvellous opportunity and the manager and me's already great mates. He'll be here any minute to collect us."

"Quite understood, Rufus," said Madoc. "Good luck and good hunting."

"Say goodbye for me to all my friends back home," said Snowy. "It's a bit of a wrench but I couldn't let Rufus take on all that work single-pawed."

"No, indeed," said Madoc. "Goodbye Snowy and good luck."

It was nice to be going home again to Wales but it was seeing the streak of gold that gave Madoc most pleasure that day, for that is what Miss Kip looked like as she sped towards her friend, tail wagging.

"Miss Kip, I'm *so* glad you're safe," said Madoc.

"And thank you, a thousand purrs," added Hamish McPurr, "for saving my Gallant 99. Without you they'd by fur coats by now."

"It was the least I could do," said Miss Kipp. "Now, thank my lucky whiskers, they've caught those villains so there won't be any more trouble from that source at any rate."

"So you managed to track them down?" asked Patchwork. "I felt sure you would."

"Brave hound," said Madoc.

"Yes," said Sam, coming up to join them, "she did a marvellous job. And she's going to get a medal for gallantry from the Queen for it."

"Oh, purr, congratulations!"

"Purr, illustrious hound!"

"Purr and thank you, you fearless animal!"

All the cats joined in their praise of Miss Kip and before Sam and the children could go home Miss Kip was persuaded to tell her story again. As she barked and growled her way through the tale all the birds of the air came and perched on the trees and on the back of the riverside benches to listen. Among them were Peter Puffin and Petula Pigeon.

"A remarkable story," said Peter to Petula when Miss Kip had finished. Only the night before he'd heard the news about the puffins and their islands and now he was so bursting with important information he swelled up to almost twice his normal size. "Yes, a remarkable story," he said again. "In fact a remarkable forty-eight hours altogether. I don't know when I've had so much to tell my colony. And just in time for the nesting season too!"

"Yes, couldn't be better," agreed Petula. "And *we're* getting some help too. Five hundred mousers and ratters are staying behind to deal with the metropolital menace. Operation Mousehunt it's called."

"Excellent," said Peter. "Now I must fly." And off he went to spread the glad tidings.

In the mysterious way that cats have, all, except of course the new Operation Mousehunt squad and Katie Cat, managed to fix up transport back to their various areas. Hamish McPurr even persuaded British Rail to lend him that famous train, the Flying Scotsman, to transport him and his fellow mousers north of the border.

On Westminster Bridge Police Constables Titch and Tuck waited to say goodbye.

"Goodbye Madoc, goodbye Patchwork. Goodbye Miss Kip and once again, thanks a million," said the two constables together.

"Purr," said Madoc.

"Purr," said Patchwork.

"Bark, bark, bark," said Miss Kip.

"Goodbye Sam, goodbye children and good luck!"

"Goodbye," called Sam and the children.

And as Sam's old van drove through Trafalgar Square the lions once again rose up on their hind legs and roared their congratulations. But when the children told their friends no one believed them.